DATA NEXUS

UNLOCKING THE FUTURE OF INSIGHTS

VIJAY PANWAR

Made with ♥ on the Notion Press Platform
www.notionpress.com

Contents

Note To Readers

Dear Reader,

As you hold this book in your hands, I want to express my gratitude for your interest in navigating the complexities of large-scale data management.

The world we live in is driven by data massive, ever-growing, and increasingly important data. Whether you're a developer, engineer, or tech enthusiast, I know first-hand the challenges you face when it comes to managing and optimizing terabyte-scale data.

It's not just about handling the data. It's about ensuring it works for you, your team, and your business in the most efficient way possible.

I've spent years honing my skills in cloud computing, SQL Server, AWS, and agile methodologies, but more importantly, I've spent years learning how to overcome the obstacles that come with big data.

My aim with this book is to provide you with not just the technical know-how, but also the insights, solutions, and strategies that will help you navigate the oceans of data we deal with today.

Let this book be your guide as you tackle the ever-evolving challenges of our data-driven world.

Sincerely,
Vijay Panwar

Preface

This book is the culmination of many years of working in the trenches of data management, software development, and cloud computing.

When I first began my journey as a software engineer, data management was simpler smaller datasets, fewer performance challenges, and simpler solutions. But as the industry evolved, so did the challenges. I found myself tackling problems that required new ways of thinking, new tools, and new methods.

Through trial and error, research and collaboration, I discovered that the key to managing large-scale data isn't just about learning the latest technologies rather it's about understanding how to use them effectively together.

SQL Server and AWS Data Lake are two such technologies that, when paired with the right strategies, provide powerful solutions for processing and managing terabyte-scale data.

In this book, you'll follow the journey of Ethan Parker, a fictional character who reflects the experiences many of us face in this field. Ethan's story is inspired by real-world challenges and real-world solutions. My hope is that through his journey, you'll find not only technical advice but also the confidence and motivation to tackle your own data challenges head-on.

I've been fortunate to work with brilliant teams, editors and mentors, and I owe much of my knowledge to those collaborations.

It's my turn to share these insights with you, so you can continue to push the boundaries of what's possible in data management.

Acknowledgements

As I reflect on the journey of bringing this book to life, I am filled with gratitude for the incredible individuals and families who have supported me along the way.

First and foremost, I want to extend my heartfelt thanks to Dennis Rilea. Your invaluable guidance, wisdom, and encouragement have been instrumental in shaping my thoughts and ideas throughout this process.

I am deeply grateful to my parents, Santosh Devi and Rajender Singh. Mom, your love and support have always been my strength. Dad, your wisdom and guidance have shaped my journey. Thank you both for always believing in me.

To my beloved wife, Poonam Vijay Panwar, your steadfast support and understanding have been my anchor. You have been there through late nights and early mornings, always believing in my vision.

I am equally grateful to my wonderful children, Viraj and Vanya, whose laughter and joy remind me of the importance of balance in life. You both inspire me every day to strive for excellence and to keep dreaming big. And to my niece, Alicia Panwar, thank you for your infectious enthusiasm and creativity, which have brightened my days.

I also want to express my deep appreciation for the Panwar family, whose encouragement has motivated me to push forward, even during challenging times. Your belief in my potential has been a constant source of strength.

I also want to thank my brother, Ajay Panwar, and his amazing wife, Ritu Panwar. Your constant support and encouragement have meant so much to me, and I'm really grateful to have both of you with me on this journey.

A special mention goes to The Business Fame and Scriberlee, whose support and platform have allowed me to share my ideas with a wider audience and fuel my aspirations in the world of business and technology.

Lastly, my sincere thanks to Ajay Bairagi and Riya Gote. Your constant support, friendship, and insights have enriched this journey and made it not only possible but also profoundly rewarding. I am grateful to have each of you in my life as I continue to explore new horizons. Thank you all for being such an essential part of this adventure!

About The Author – Vijay Panwar

Vijay Panwar is a highly experienced software engineer with over 11 years in the technology sector, making significant contributions to the field through his expertise and innovative approach. He earned his Master's degree in Computer Science from San Francisco Bay University in Fremont, CA, in 2016, graduating with an outstanding 4.0 GPA—a testament to his dedication and mastery of the subject.

Vijay's technical proficiency encompasses a diverse array of technologies, including Python, SQL Server, AWS services, and microservices architecture. This broad skill set empowers him to address complex challenges in software development and data management effectively. He has a proven track record of optimizing big data processing and enhancing database performance, with several published research papers that have garnered attention in both academic and professional circles.

In recognition of his knowledge and contributions to the industry, Vijay was invited to speak at the prestigious MySQL Summit in 2024. This opportunity allowed him to share his insights and experiences with fellow professionals, further solidifying his reputation as a thought leader in the tech community.

Driven by a passion for innovation and a strong commitment to lifelong learning, Vijay continually seeks to harness the transformative power of technology to enhance efficiency and improve systems. His work not only showcases his technical prowess but also reflects his visionary outlook on the future of data and software engineering, inspiring others to push the boundaries of what is possible in this ever-evolving landscape.

I'm always happy to hear from you. You can reach me at vijaypanwar.author@gmail.com

The Dawn Of Data Oceans

Have you ever felt overwhelmed by the sheer volume of data you have to manage? Let me tell YOU - You're not alone.

In today's fast-paced digital world, data isn't just a by-product of business! But it's the lifeblood.

Every click, every transaction, every interaction generates data, and it's growing at an unprecedented rate. But as exciting as it is to have access to so much information, it can also be daunting.

Let me ask you –

- How do you keep up with the flood of data coming at you every second?
- How do you ensure that your systems can handle it all without breaking a sweat?

This is the challenge that many of us face in the tech industry. The data keeps coming, and we need to find ways to store it, process it, and make sense of it — all without losing our sanity.

Whether you're dealing with real-time data from a live chat application, a train network system, or massive historical datasets, the demands on your infrastructure are only getting bigger. The question isn't just how to survive in this data deluge, but how to thrive.

Enter SQL Server and AWS Data Lake — two powerful tools that, when used together, can help you master the art of large-scale data management.

SQL Server is your go-to for handling structured data with precision and reliability. It's like the sturdy ship that keeps you afloat in the data ocean. AWS Data Lake, on the other hand, is the flexible, scalable solution that allows you to store and analyze data in all its forms, structured or unstructured. It's like having a vast, open sea where you can navigate and explore without limits.

Now you'll ask me - why are these tools so important? Because they provide the foundation for managing terabyte-scale data efficiently. They help you avoid common pitfalls like performance bottlenecks, data loss, and runaway costs. And they're not just for the tech giants, but businesses of all sizes can leverage these technologies to gain a competitive edge.

To make all of this more relatable, let's step into the shoes of someone who's been there, done that. Meet Ethan Parker, a Senior Software Engineer working in the USA. Like many of us, Ethan started his career managing small datasets, but over time, he found himself grappling with increasingly complex data challenges. Today, he's on the front lines of data management, dealing with live data streams, massive databases, and the ever-present need to scale.

Through Ethan's experiences, we'll explore the real-world challenges and solutions that come with managing terabyte-scale data. Whether you're a seasoned data professional or just starting out, Ethan's journey will resonate with you. He's faced the same frustrations, the same late-night troubleshooting sessions, and the same moments of triumph that come with finally getting it right.

So, if you've ever found yourself staring at a screen full of data, wondering how you're going to make it all work, this book is for you.

Together, we'll dive into the deep end of data management, learning the tools and techniques that can help you turn an overwhelming challenge into an opportunity for innovation and growth!

I wish you luck and success!

Meet The Characters & The Core Concepts

Before diving into the technical depths of this book, let's take a moment to meet the key players and the concepts that will guide us through the journey of advanced data handling with AWS Data Lake and SQL Server.

The Characters

Character 1: Ethan

The Strategist – A data visionary with a sharp eye for scalable solutions and a heart for leading the team through any storm. Our main protagonist, Ethan is the team leader with a sharp focus on solving complex data challenges. With years of experience in managing terabyte- scale data, he is known for his pragmatic approach and ability to simplify the most complicated concepts. Ethan believes in leading by example and often draws on real-world cases to bring the team together and tackle obstacles.

Character 2: Jake

The Tech-Savvy Joker – Master of data engineering with a knack for keeping the room light, even when the data is heavy. The lively and often humorous data engineer who brings energy to the team. While Jake loves cracking jokes, he is equally skilled in deep data integration and processing. His playful banter hides a sharp mind that's always ahead of the curve in the latest tech trends. Expect Jake to be the one who asks the questions you might be too afraid to ask but are thinking.

Character 3: Emily

Beauty with Brains – A brilliant data scientist who effortlessly balances AI, machine learning, and real-world applications. A no-nonsense data scientist, Emily is the voice of reason in the team. She's all about practicality and efficiency. With her deep knowledge of AI and machine learning, Emily plays a vital role in creating actionable insights from raw data. Her ability to explain complex concepts in layman's terms makes her an invaluable resource.

Character 4: Sarah

The Heart of the Team – Ethan's anchor, offering wisdom and perspective, keeping him grounded in both life and tech. Ethan's partner and emotional anchor, Sarah provides the personal perspective needed to humanize the technical world of data management. Her role in the book may seem peripheral, but her conversations with Ethan help him reflect on the broader implications of the technology he works with, offering readers a balance between technical mastery and personal fulfillment.

Core Concepts

AWS Data Lake

At the heart of modern data strategy, AWS Data Lake is the foundation of this book. It enables businesses to store vast amounts of structured and unstructured data in a central repository. With services like S3 for storage, Glue for data cataloging, and Athena for querying, the data lake architecture allows real-time analytics and machine learning directly on raw data.

SQL Server

While AWS offers cloud scalability, SQL Server remains a powerful on-premise option for managing relational databases. The integration of SQL Server with AWS Data Lake forms the backbone of many discussions in this book, particularly in managing terabyte-scale data efficiently.

AI and Machine Learning

As the book progresses, AI-driven data analytics becomes a recurring theme. Ethan and his team explore how AI and machine learning can unlock deeper insights from data, automate decision-making, and improve performance at scale.

Cost Management

A critical challenge in any data strategy, the book will frequently revisit the topic of cost management. By comparing traditional on-premise solutions with cloud-based AWS services, the team explores how to manage and optimize costs without compromising performance.

Security

In an age where data breaches and cyber threats are rampant, this book doesn't shy away from tackling data security concerns. We'll explore real-world examples of how major institutions handle security risks in cloud environments, and how AWS's security features provide a robust defence.

The Journey Ahead

Throughout the book, these characters will not only guide us through technical scenarios but will also engage in thought-provoking conversations and discussions that humanize the world of data science. Whether it's over a team dinner or a late-night reflection with Sarah, the balance of technology and humanity will always be at the forefront.

As we begin, ask yourself: How do you plan to integrate the future of data into your own world? The journey ahead will help you answer that.

CHAPTER I

Ethan's World

Ethan Parker had always been a man of precision, driven by an innate curiosity to unravel the complexities of the digital world. As a Senior Data Architect at one of the leading global tech companies in the USA, he thrived on the challenges of big data.

Ethan's office was a reflection of his meticulously organized mind. Every detail, from the sleek glass desk to the precisely arranged monitors, exuded an air of calm control. The room was designed with a minimalist touch. White walls, devoid of unnecessary decoration, and shelves that held only the essentials - a few technical manuals, some data architecture references, and his favorite coding books.

No clutter, no distractions.

The soft hum of his high-powered workstation was the only sound breaking the silence, a subtle reminder of the powerful technology at his disposal.

His dual monitors, always perfectly aligned, displayed endless streams of data, logs, and scripts. One screen was dedicated to the SQL Server dashboards, showing real-time performance metrics and server health. The other often displayed his AWS management console, providing him a bird's-eye view of their cloud infrastructure. His system was configured with precision, allowing him to dive deep into complex datasets with a few swift keystrokes.Ethan's workspace was engineered for efficiency, much like his problem-solving approach. Every piece of technology, from the latest ergonomic chair to the standing desk converter, was selected with purpose — designed to support long hours of concentrated work.

Even the lighting in the room was carefully curated - soft yet bright enough to keep him alert during late-night troubleshooting sessions.

Above all, the space embodied his disciplined mindset. Just as he approached coding and data management with structure and clarity, his office left no room for chaos. It was a sanctuary for focus, a place where Ethan could sift through mountains of data, solve complex problems, and make the precise decisions that defined his role as a Senior Data Architect.

This methodical setup wasn't just for productivity — it was a physical manifestation of how Ethan viewed the world. Everything had a place, everything had a purpose, and with the right approach, even the most overwhelming data challenges could be unraveled.

Over the years, Ethan had climbed the ranks from being a software engineer, where he first dipped his hands into the chaotic world of data management, to now leading critical projects that dealt with the terabytes of data flowing through the system every day.

But despite his professional achievements, it was the quieter moments in his personal life that kept him grounded. His wife, Sarah, a practical yet empathetic woman, had become his anchor in a sea of data-driven chaos.

Their relationship was a unique mix of love and understanding. Sarah, though not from the tech world herself, had come to appreciate the world Ethan operated in.

Their dinner conversations often meandered into discussions about his latest data management struggles or new cloud integration initiatives. Sarah would listen intently, occasionally asking questions or offering her layman's perspective, which Ethan often found surprisingly insightful.

One evening, as Ethan arrived home after a particularly grueling day at the office, he found Sarah seated by the window, a cup of coffee in hand. "Long day?" she asked, sensing his exhaustion without him needing to say a word. He nodded, sinking into the couch beside her.

“SQL Server's giving us hell again,” Ethan said, shaking his head in frustration. “We're trying to scale for real-time data processing, but it's reaching its limit. Every time we restart the service, there's a risk of losing data.”

As he spoke, the weight of the challenges they faced loomed large in the room. SQL Server had always been a reliable workhorse for their data management needs, but as the organization expanded and the volume of incoming data surged, it became increasingly apparent that the traditional relational database was struggling to keep up.

The demands for real-time analytics were mounting; teams needed immediate access to data to make informed decisions, and SQL Server, while robust, was not designed for the scale they were now operating at.

With each system restart, which had become a frequent necessity due to performance issues, the potential for data loss felt like a ticking time bomb. They couldn't afford to lose vital insights or operational data that were crucial for running their business efficiently.

The limitations were further exacerbated by the nature of their data, which was not only growing in volume but also diversifying in format. From structured data in traditional databases to unstructured data from IoT devices and social media interactions, the sheer complexity was overwhelming. Ethan knew that sticking with SQL Server in its current state could jeopardize their competitive edge.

He could see the team's concern reflected in their faces. "We need to explore scalable solutions," he urged, knowing they had to consider options like AWS Data Lake that could accommodate the terabyte-scale data handling required for their future growth. The realization that they might have to transition from their long-standing database system to a more modern, cloud-based architecture was daunting but necessary.

"Let's start by analyzing how we can integrate more flexible, scalable solutions while ensuring that our data integrity and availability remain intact," he continued, determined to turn their struggles into a stepping stone for innovation. The path ahead was fraught with challenges, but with a proactive approach, they could harness the power of emerging technologies to navigate the complexities of modern data management.

Sarah raised an eyebrow. "Isn't there some way to back it up before restarting?"

Ethan smiled. "It's not that simple, but you're on the right track. We need something that can scale without losing the data in transit. Maybe something more cloud-based. I don't know... it's a lot to think through."

In moments like these, he found clarity. While Sarah didn't understand every technical detail, her ability to simplify the problem often gave Ethan the perspective he needed. It was this balance — his life at home and his challenges at work — that shaped Ethan's approach to his career. He wasn't just solving data problems for the sake of it. He was trying to create a system that worked seamlessly, so the pressures of work wouldn't follow him home anymore.

At the office, Ethan's team reflected the diversity of personalities and skill sets that made their work so dynamic.

Emily Carter, the company's seasoned database administrator, was a woman whose presence commanded attention without her even trying. With her tall frame and sharp, angular features, she carried herself with a natural authority, often highlighted by her straightforward style. Her hair, a deep chestnut brown streaked with threads of silver, was always tied back in a no-nonsense bun. Her look was practical, much like her work ethic function over flair, but always professional.

Her workstation reflected this history. Unlike Ethan's sleek, minimalistic setup, Emily's desk was cluttered with stacks of papers, system diagrams, and Post-it notes scribbled with SQL queries and error codes. Her monitors, three of them arranged in a semicircle, were filled with blinking dashboards and rows of code.

She was always in the middle of something — whether it was troubleshooting a performance issue or running complex queries to optimize their databases. Even in the chaos, there was a method to her madness. Every paper had its place, and every note was part of a larger mental map she carried with her, a deep understanding of the systems that had evolved under her watch.

Emily's brilliance was undeniable.

She could pinpoint the root of a server bottleneck within minutes or predict when a system needed an upgrade before it became a problem. But her years of experience had come at a cost. She was overworked, often the first one in the office and the last to leave, with her evenings spent responding to urgent messages and troubleshooting late-night issues. She was the backbone of the data infrastructure, and she knew it, even if it meant burning herself out to keep things running.

To the younger engineers, Emily was a mentor, a wealth of knowledge always ready to share her expertise. But there was a guardedness to her as well — a wariness that came from years of having to fix problems others created. She had seen it all, from minor glitches to full-blown system crashes, and it had made her cautious, maybe even a little cynical. While others saw the cloud and cutting-edge solutions as the future, Emily often viewed them with scepticism, preferring tried-and-tested methods over flashy new tech.

Still, there was no denying her loyalty to the company and her dedication to keeping everything running smoothly. To Ethan, she was an invaluable asset, someone he could rely on when things got tough, even if their approaches differed.

While he thrived on innovation and efficiency, Emily was the guardian of stability, the one who ensured that no matter what new tech was introduced, the foundation remained unshakable.

Emily had a deep understanding of SQL Server, but even she admitted they were pushing the boundaries of what their current infrastructure could handle. Her desk, usually cluttered with printouts of database schemas and performance reports, was often a scene of frantic activity as she juggled multiple fires at once.

Then there was Jake Thompson, the newest addition to the team — a fresh-faced cloud engineer with an infectious enthusiasm that brightened even the most mundane tasks. With his tousled sandy hair, casual jeans, and tech-branded hoodie, Jake exuded the energy of someone just starting his career, eager to make his mark.

His curiosity seemed boundless, always asking questions and soaking up every piece of knowledge that Ethan and Emily shared about large-scale data operations.

What he lacked in experience, he made up for in sheer determination and a willingness to learn, staying late to experiment with new cloud architectures and meticulously studying best practices for scaling systems.

Jake's youthful drive and openness to new ideas brought a refreshing contrast to the team's dynamics, making him a vibrant catalyst for innovation. Unlike Emily, who grounded her strategies in years of industry experience and pragmatic problem-solving, Jake's approach was marked by an infectious enthusiasm that encouraged the team to think outside the box.

His willingness to embrace the latest trends in technology, such as machine learning and AI, invigorated discussions, pushing the boundaries of conventional thought and inspiring his colleagues to explore uncharted territories.

While Emily's seasoned pragmatism often ensured that the team remained anchored in reality—evaluating risks, understanding limitations, and maintaining a clear focus on their objectives—Jake's youthful exuberance acted like a breath of fresh air. He often reminded them of the possibilities that lay beyond the immediate challenges they faced.

His enthusiasm was palpable; it fueled brainstorming sessions where even the most unconventional ideas were welcomed and explored without judgment. This openness fostered a culture of creativity that made the team more resilient and adaptable in a fast- paced, ever-evolving tech landscape.

Ethan, with his methodical approach, balanced the team's dynamics by providing structure and a clear roadmap. He valued Jake's innovative ideas but also recognized the importance of Emily's experienced insights.

This interplay created a harmonious synergy where ideas could be born, evaluated, and refined. Jake's burst of energy often sparked lively debates that encouraged the entire team to engage deeply with each concept. His youthful spirit not only inspired a sense of camaraderie but also pushed them all to be bolder in their thinking, embracing experimentation and iterative processes as they worked through complex projects.

Together, the trio formed a unique blend of perspectives.

Jake's youthful drive infused the team with optimism and a sense of possibility, Emily's pragmatic wisdom ensured that they stayed grounded and focused on deliverables, while Ethan's methodical planning provided the necessary framework to transform innovative ideas into actionable strategies.

This rich tapestry of approaches not only made their collaboration enjoyable but also elevated the quality of their work, setting the stage for groundbreaking solutions in their field. In every meeting, every discussion, and every brainstorming session, Jake's energy served as a reminder that innovation thrives when different viewpoints come together, paving the way for a future full of potential and promise.

Jake's energy was contagious, even if his lack of experience sometimes led to rookie mistakes. Ethan saw a younger version of himself in Jake — eager, ambitious, and slightly overwhelmed by the complexities of the job.

Mark Davis, on the other hand, was a different story. The IT manager, skeptical of new technologies and even more so of cloud migration, had been with the company for years. Mark approached every new proposal with caution, preferring the stability of their legacy systems over the uncertain waters of AWS Data Lakes and cloud-based solutions.

Ethan respected Mark's experience, but their discussions were often a tug-of-war between innovation and the tried-and-tested methods that had kept the company running for so long.

As Ethan sat in his office late one afternoon, reviewing the latest performance metrics, he thought about the meeting scheduled for the next day. They would need to address the growing concerns over the system's ability to process live data without downtime.

Mark would likely argue for another round of SQL optimizations, while

Jake would eagerly suggest moving everything to AWS. Emily would back whichever solution could ease the load on her team the fastest.

Ethan felt the weight of the decision bearing down on him. Balancing the caution of experience with the need to innovate was a constant struggle. But deep down, he knew they were running out of time. The data was only getting bigger, and their current setup was already creaking under the pressure. They needed a new approach—one that would not only scale but ensure the integrity of their live data in real time.

As he closed his laptop and leaned back in his chair, Ethan couldn't help but think of the conversation he'd had with Sarah the night before. They had been sitting on the rooftop of their favorite bar, the city skyline glittering against the twilight sky, when she had shared her perspective on problem-solving. "There's always a solution," she'd said, her voice calm and reassuring, "even if it isn't immediately obvious."

Her words resonated deeply with him now. The complexities of his professional life were beginning to feel overwhelming. He had spent countless hours sifting through data logs and troubleshooting issues with SQL Server, grappling with its limitations while trying to lead his team toward more efficient data management solutions. As the manager, he had to be the anchor for his team, guiding them through challenges and uncertainty, even when his own confidence wavered.

Balancing the needs of his team with the relentless demands of the system was no easy task. He knew that his team was feeling the pressure, too—long nights spent troubleshooting, the constant worry about data loss during system restarts, and the urgent need for scalable solutions weighed heavily on their shoulders. He was aware that they looked to him for guidance and support, and the responsibility to foster a productive and positive environment felt immense.

Yet, in that moment of reflection, he felt a flicker of determination igniting within him. Sarah's words reminded him that every obstacle could be reframed as an opportunity. Solutions were often hidden in the complexities they faced. It was a matter of stepping back, examining the landscape from different angles, and engaging the collective wisdom of his team.

Ethan took a deep breath, grounding himself in the present. He envisioned the brainstorming session ahead, where he could facilitate discussions that might lead to innovative ideas. He thought about bringing in fresh perspectives, perhaps exploring AWS Data Lake, and creating a plan that could transform their data management strategies.

In the whirlwind of technology and data demands, he understood that maintaining open communication and collaboration would be key to overcoming these hurdles. With a newfound resolve, Ethan prepared to navigate the complexities ahead, knowing that with patience, creativity, and teamwork, they could chart a course toward success.

One thing was certain - the next chapter of their data journey was about to begin, and it would be one that none of them could afford to get wrong.

CHAPTER II

Facing the Data Deluge

Ethan sat at his desk, staring at the endless flow of data flashing on his monitor. It felt like a flood, constantly pouring in, and even with all his experience, the sheer amount was overwhelming.

The company had recently experienced a significant surge in new customers, a development that was exciting and promising. However, this influx brought with it a massive increase in data — an unforeseen challenge that quickly became overwhelming. Their current systems, which had been cobbled together over time with various temporary solutions and quick fixes, were now buckling under the pressure.

Each new customer added to the flood of data, stretching the limits of their infrastructure. What had once been manageable was now a mountain of information that their systems struggled to process efficiently.

The patchwork of upgrades and quick fixes that had kept the system running in the past were now showing their limitations, struggling to maintain performance and stability as the data demands grew exponentially.

Ethan leaned back in his chair, massaging his temples, feeling the pressure build. It wasn't just about managing the data anymore. It was about finding a way to handle it smoothly, without pushing their fragile system to the breaking point.

As the sun dipped low, casting a warm glow over his home office, Ethan closed his laptop and headed downstairs. The scent of dinner greeted him, and he found Sarah, his wife, busy in the kitchen.

She turned, offering him a soft smile, but her eyes quickly narrowed with concern when she saw the weariness in his face.

"Tough day?" she asked, setting down a pan.

"Data deluge," Ethan sighed, sitting at the kitchen island. "We've acquired a ton of new customers, which is great for the business, but the data... it's overwhelming. Our current system is creaking under the pressure."

Sarah wiped her hands on a dish towel and leaned on the counter, listening intently as she always did when he spoke about work. "Isn't that what you've been preparing for? Scaling up?"

"In theory, yes. But the reality is more complicated. We're using SQL Server to handle everything right now, but with the influx, it's starting to slow down. Every restart, every hiccup, means a risk of losing data. And we can't afford that — not at this scale. I've been thinking about introducing AWS Data Lake into the mix, but it's not an easy transition. Emily's skeptical, and Mark's... well, he's Mark."

Sarah chuckled softly. "Let me guess — he doesn't like change?"

"Exactly. He's cautious, especially with anything cloud-based. Emily's the backbone of the SQL Server infrastructure, so any change is going to be a tough sell. But we need a solution — fast."

Sarah tilted her head, considering. "You always figure it out. It's what you do." Ethan smiled. "Let's hope I can this time."

The next morning, Ethan gathered with the team in the conference room. Emily sat in her usual spot, already reviewing performance logs, her expression a mix of frustration and concentration. Across from her sat Jake, his eager eyes darting between his notebook and the whiteboard as he scribbled notes in anticipation. Mark Davis, the IT manager, leaned back in his chair with his arms crossed, his skepticism palpable even before the meeting began.

Ethan cleared his throat, bringing the room to attention. "Alright, team. We've got a serious problem. As you all know, with the recent customer acquisitions, the amount of data coming in has tripled. Our SQL Server is struggling, and we're hitting bottlenecks in processing live data. If we don't scale up, we're going to start losing data every time the service restarts."

Emily nodded, her fingers tapping her keyboard. “I’ve noticed the slowdowns, especially during peak traffic. It’s only going to get worse. But switching systems isn’t something we can just do overnight.”

Ethan turned to Jake, who had been practically buzzing with ideas. “Jake, thoughts on bringing AWS Data Lake into the mix?”

Jake sat up straighter, excitement lighting up his face. “Honestly, it’s the perfect solution for this kind of scale. We can offload a huge portion of the data into the lake and use it as a staging area before processing it with SQL. It’ll ease the load and allow for better data ingestion. Plus, it integrates well with cloud storage solutions.”

Emily raised an eyebrow. “And what about security? Moving all that data to the cloud comes with its own set of risks.”

“True,” Jake conceded. “But AWS has built-in encryption and access control mechanisms. It’s secure, and it’ll give us the flexibility we need.”

Mark shifted in his seat. “I’m still not sold on this cloud idea. We’ve managed with SQL Server for years. Moving to AWS feels like jumping into the deep end without checking if the water’s safe.”

Ethan leaned forward, addressing Mark’s concerns head-on. “I get it, Mark. I know you’re cautious, and rightfully so. But the reality is, SQL Server alone can’t handle what’s coming. We’re already seeing the cracks, and AWS Data Lake can bridge that gap. We can’t afford to keep patching things up.”

There was a pause as Mark considered this, his face tight with thought.

Emily finally spoke, her voice calm but firm, cutting through the tension in the room. "I’m not against the idea of moving to the cloud, but we need a clear and detailed plan. This process isn’t as simple as flipping a switch and transferring everything over. The transition needs to be meticulously planned to avoid any data loss. We’re talking about moving vast amounts of critical information; any misstep could lead to significant gaps or corruptions in our data. We need to ensure that every piece of data is accounted for and safely transferred, with thorough checks and balances in place to prevent any loss during the migration."

She continued, emphasizing the importance of stability. "It's also crucial that we maintain system stability throughout the transition. We don't want to find ourselves in a situation where the new system introduces more issues than it solves. The goal is to improve our data handling, not to end up with more problems. We need a strategy that not only addresses the immediate challenges but also ensures a smooth and reliable operation once the migration is complete. In short, we must approach this with a solid plan that considers both the technical and practical aspects to avoid creating new headaches while solving the old ones."

Ethan nodded, appreciating her pragmatism. "Agreed. We'll take it step by step. The goal is to create a hybrid system—SQL Server for the critical live data we can't afford to lose, and AWS Data Lake to handle the overflow. We can start by migrating non-essential data first, and once we're comfortable with the process, we scale from there."

Jake grinned, already scribbling down the action plan. "I'm in. Let's do this."

Mark finally relented with a sigh. "Alright. But I'm keeping a close eye on this. If anything goes sideways..."

"We'll handle it," Ethan assured him. "This is about being proactive, not reactive. The data isn't going to stop coming, and we need to be ready for the future."

As the meeting ended, Ethan leaned back in his chair, gathering his thoughts.

He had a lot to explain, and he knew the challenges ahead were significant. "It's not just about fixing what's broken," he began, speaking as if to someone who might not be entirely familiar with the technical details. "We need to think bigger, to prepare for the future, not just the present."

He continued, "Take scaling operations for example. It's like trying to expand a highway to handle more traffic. We can either make the existing road wider — that's called vertical scaling — or build new lanes alongside the old ones, which is horizontal scaling. For us, the horizontal approach makes more sense. We'll use cloud services to add servers on demand. It's faster, more flexible, and it won't put too much strain on any one part of the system."

Ethan paused, his mind turning to the bigger picture. "We're not just solving today's problem; we're future-proofing the whole infrastructure. That means building something that can handle not only the data we have now but also what's coming in the future. Cloud technologies like AWS will allow us to scale up or down without having to overhaul everything every time we grow."

He rubbed his temples and smiled slightly. "And then there's the data storms—that's what I call the constant flood of information coming our way. Every new customer brings a massive amount of data, and it just keeps piling up. We have to make sure we're not just reacting to it but are ready for it. It's like standing on the shore and seeing a storm on the horizon. You can't stop it, but you can build stronger defenses."

He leaned forward, ready to explain more. "One way to do that is by using an AWS Data Lake. It's different from a regular database. Instead of trying to organize everything perfectly upfront, we can store the data in its raw form and figure out how to use it later. It's flexible, which means we don't have to worry about future data breaking the system."

Ethan knew that optimization was key to making everything run smoothly. "We also have to think about optimization. It's not enough to just throw more resources at the problem. We need to be smart about how we handle data. For example, we'll review the SQL queries and make sure they're written efficiently. Sometimes, just changing the way we ask for data can cut the processing time in half. We'll also use something called data partitioning, which is like splitting a huge book into smaller chapters so it's easier to find what you're looking for."

He felt a renewed sense of purpose as he wrapped up his explanation. "It's going to be a tough road, but we have a plan. We're not just reacting to problems; we're preparing for the future. By scaling the right way, optimizing where it counts, and building a system that can handle any storm, we'll be ready—not just for today, but for whatever comes next."

As Ethan finished explaining the plan, he looked around the room at his team, each face reflecting a mix of determination and apprehension. They were on the brink of a major transformation, poised to tackle the data challenges head-on.

But as the meeting concluded, Ethan knew that implementing these changes would bring its own set of hurdles. The real test lay ahead: integrating new systems into their daily operations and making them work seamlessly. With the groundwork laid, it was time to delve into the specifics of how they would turn their ambitious plans into reality. What steps would be needed to completely update their data systems and guarantee smooth, real-time processing?

CHAPTER III

Expanding the Data Horizons

The meeting room buzzed with the low hum of conversation as Ethan's team gathered. The tension was palpable.

The room's large screen displayed a real-time data stream from their new customer acquisition platform — a live chat application used by millions. It was chaotic, with data flowing in faster than they could process it, causing intermittent freezes and system slowdowns.

Ethan's gaze was locked onto the screen, his mind a whirlwind of thoughts and calculations. The screen displayed an endless cascade of data streams, their chaotic flow a stark reminder of the magnitude of their problem.

Each flicker of red error messages and each delay in the real-time updates felt like a jarring siren, alerting him to the system's vulnerabilities. The pressure of the situation weighed heavily on him, not just as a leader but as someone deeply invested in the success of the project.

His thoughts raced, analyzing every aspect of the system's current setup. He mentally reviewed the strategies they had considered, weighing their potential impacts. Could they implement sharding effectively? How would the integration with AWS RDS work out in practice? The questions buzzed in his head like persistent flies, each one demanding an answer. His usual calm demeanor was challenged by the urgency of the moment, making him acutely aware of the critical nature of their next steps.

The atmosphere in the room was thick with anticipation. Emily, Jake, and Mark watched him closely, their expressions a mix of concern and hope. They were all counting on Ethan to guide them through this crisis.

Mark's skeptical gaze, Emily's tired but focused eyes, and Jake's eager but anxious face added to the pressure Ethan felt. He knew that any decision made today would ripple through their entire system and affect every one of them.

Ethan's heart pounded as he considered the potential consequences of their actions—or inactions. He could almost feel the weight of the data crashing down on their infrastructure, a tidal wave threatening to overwhelm their defenses.

He was keenly aware that the success of their project depended on their ability to act swiftly and effectively, and he had to remain composed and decisive. His mind worked tirelessly, crafting a plan that could turn the tide and prevent a full-blown system collapse.

He started the meeting by diving into the core of the issue: scalability. "Scalability isn't just a buzzword," Ethan began, his tone serious but calm. "It's about adapting our system to handle increased loads without breaking down. Think of it like expanding a highway to accommodate more traffic. In our case, the 'highway' is our SQL Server, and the 'traffic' is the data we're processing."

Ethan explained that their current system, though robust, was nearing its limits.

They needed to leverage AWS RDS (Relational Database Service) to scale efficiently. "AWS RDS lets us expand our database capacity without the headaches of managing physical hardware," he said. "It allows us to add more database instances as our data grows. We can start with smaller, more manageable units and scale up seamlessly as needed. This approach ensures that we're ready for the spikes in data volume, like those seen in a real-time chat application where messages are constantly being sent and received."

Emily, who had been listening intently, finally spoke. "Scaling is crucial, but it's not just about adding resources. It's also about ensuring that the system remains stable and data is not lost during the scaling process. I've dealt with too many instances where quick fixes led to more issues later on."

Ethan nodded, understanding her concerns. "Absolutely, Emily. That's why we're also implementing best practices for handling live data. For instance, using sharding to distribute data across multiple servers can help manage the load. Sharding divides the data into smaller, more manageable pieces, reducing the strain on any single server and improving performance."

To illustrate his point, Ethan shared a recent success story. "Let me give you a real-world example," he said, pulling up a case study on the screen. "We had a similar challenge with a real-time communication system for a major client. They needed to handle thousands of concurrent users, and the existing setup was struggling. We migrated their system to AWS RDS, implemented sharding, and used automated backups to ensure data integrity. The result? Seamless processing with zero data loss, even during server restarts."

Jake, the young cloud engineer, was taking notes furiously. Ethan saw an opportunity to mentor him. "Jake," he said, addressing the eager engineer, "scalability isn't just about technical setups. It's about understanding the demands of your application and planning accordingly. For real-time systems, it's crucial to ensure low latency and high availability. You'll need to get comfortable with concepts like load balancing and failover strategies."

Jake nodded, his eyes wide with a mixture of excitement and determination. "I'll make sure to dive into those concepts," he replied.

Emily, clearly relieved to be working with a proactive team, looked at Ethan. "This plan sounds solid, but we'll need to monitor everything closely as we implement it. The last thing we want is to introduce new issues while fixing old ones."

Ethan agreed. "Monitoring will be key. We'll set up comprehensive tracking to ensure that everything works as planned and to catch any issues before they escalate."

From a technical perspective, Ethan's statement highlighted the crucial role that monitoring plays in maintaining system integrity and performance, especially when dealing with large- scale data operations. Comprehensive tracking involves implementing various monitoring tools and strategies to continuously oversee the health and functionality of the system.

Firstly, Ethan planned to employ real-time performance monitoring tools. These tools provide live data on how different components of their infrastructure are performing, including server load, database query response times, and network latency.

For instance, using AWS CloudWatch or similar services, they could set up dashboards that display critical metrics in real-time. This would allow them to keep an eye on how their SQL Server and AWS RDS instances are handling the incoming data loads, ensuring that any performance degradation is detected immediately.

Additionally, error and log management would be a significant part of their monitoring strategy. By aggregating and analyzing log files from various sources—such as application logs, database logs, and system logs—they could identify patterns or anomalies that might indicate underlying issues. For example, if there were unexpected spikes in error rates or latency, these logs would provide insights into what went wrong and help pinpoint the root cause.

Ethan also emphasized the importance of setting up alerts and automated notifications. These alerts would be configured to trigger under specific conditions, such as when system resource usage exceeds predefined thresholds or when error rates surpass acceptable limits. By receiving immediate notifications, the team could respond swiftly to any issues before they have a chance to escalate into more severe problems.

They would implement health checks and performance benchmarks regularly. Health checks involve running periodic tests to ensure that all system components are functioning correctly, while performance benchmarks help evaluate how the system performs under different loads. This ongoing evaluation would help them understand their system's behavior in various scenarios and make necessary adjustments to optimize performance.

Ethan's approach to monitoring was about creating a safety net that would catch potential issues early and ensure that the system remained robust and responsive. It was about being proactive rather than reactive—anticipating problems before they became critical and maintaining a stable, high-performing data infrastructure.

As the meeting drew to a close, the conference room's bright lights cast a warm glow over the team. The once tense atmosphere, charged with uncertainty and the weight of impending decisions, now felt lighter and more hopeful.

Ethan leaned back in his chair, his posture relaxed and his face reflecting a renewed sense of confidence. The whiteboard, previously scrawled with hastily drawn diagrams and lists of challenges, now featured a neatly organized roadmap outlining their strategy. The clutter of sticky notes and scribbled figures had been replaced with clear, actionable steps, a testament to their collective brainstorming and problem-solving.

The team members, having absorbed the gravity of the discussions, now looked more assured. Emily, whose usual furrowed brow had softened, gave Ethan a nod of approval. Her exhaustion from the ongoing data issues was momentarily forgotten as she recognized the clarity and direction they now had.

Jake's eyes sparkled with a mix of relief and excitement; the solutions proposed were not just theoretical but actionable and well within their grasp. Even Mark, who had remained cautious throughout the meeting, appeared more optimistic, his earlier skepticism tempered by the solid plan that had emerged.

Ethan's mind raced through the steps they would take in the coming weeks: setting up the enhanced monitoring systems, deploying the scalable architecture, and integrating the new data processing strategies.

He felt a surge of anticipation at the thought of tackling these tasks, driven by a clear vision of what needed to be done. The feeling of impending action was palpable; it was as if the heavy cloud of uncertainty that had hovered over them was lifting, revealing a path forward bathed in sunlight.

The meeting room, once a battleground of ideas and concerns, had transformed into a launchpad for their new strategy. Ethan glanced around at his team, their faces now illuminated by the soft glow of the room's lights, and felt a profound sense of optimism.

They weren't just expanding their capabilities - they were fortifying their defenses against future challenges. The sense of camaraderie and shared purpose was almost tangible, a unifying force that promised to propel them toward success.

As they gathered their notes and prepared to leave, Ethan's mind was already turning to the next steps. He knew the journey ahead would be demanding, but the clarity they had achieved provided a strong foundation.

The excitement of turning plans into action, of overcoming obstacles, and of setting new benchmarks invigorated him. With a final, satisfied look at the whiteboard and a quiet, resolute nod to himself, Ethan felt ready to face whatever lay ahead.

The real work was just beginning, but for now, there was a palpable sense of achievement and a clear vision of the road to come.

CHAPTER IV

The Pursuit of Performance

The office was buzzing with a frenetic energy that mirrored the growing demands on their systems. Ethan sat at his desk, staring at the metrics displayed on his screen. Every peak in traffic told the same story: the system was under strain. It was as if their live data processing system, which had always been reliable, was now buckling under the weight of their success.

The incoming flood of customer data was not just a wave — *it was a tsunami.*

As the numbers continued to rise, Ethan's phone buzzed. A message from Mark appeared on the screen: "Meeting in five. We need to talk about these performance dips."

Ethan sighed. He knew what was coming. The conversation wouldn't just be about the technical aspects - there would be the inevitable debate about cost vs. benefit! Something Mark was always cautious about.

Ethan gathered his thoughts as he made his way to the conference room. The walls, adorned with motivational posters that always seemed a bit out of place in a tech company, did little to lighten his mood.

Today, even the coffee machine seemed to be working against him, sputtering in protest as he filled his cup.

Inside the meeting room, Emily was already seated, looking tired but focused, her fingers tapping out a rhythm on the table. Jake sat next to her, wide-eyed and ready, notebook in hand. Mark, as expected, sat at the head of the table, his expression a mix of impatience and skepticism.

Ethan sat down and opened the discussion. "Alright, we've seen the numbers. We're hitting performance bottlenecks during peak traffic times, and the live data processing isn't keeping up. We need to optimize the system before it breaks."

Mark leaned forward, arms crossed. “Optimization always sounds great, Ethan, but let’s not forget that this is going to cost — time and money. What’s your plan, and how do we keep it reasonable?”

Ethan expected the pushback. "We’re not talking about a full overhaul," he said, voice steady. "We’ll start with SQL Server. There are a few steps we can take that don’t require a massive investment but can make a huge difference."

Jake chimed in, eager to contribute. "Indexing, right? I’ve read that can speed up queries by a lot."

Ethan nodded, appreciating the enthusiasm. "Exactly. Indexing is like giving the system a roadmap. Instead of scanning the entire database to find what it needs, it goes straight to the information. Think of it like trying to find a book in a library—without an index, you’d have to search every shelf."

Emily added, "But if we over-index, we could slow things down in other areas, like insert and update operations."

"Right," Ethan agreed. "That’s why we need to be strategic. We focus on the queries that are being run most often during peak times—those are the ones we optimize."

Mark, unconvinced, leaned back in his chair. "That’s just one step. Is it really going to solve the problem?"

Ethan sighed inwardly but kept his tone calm. "It’s just the start. We also need to look at partitioning."

Jake’s hand shot up. “Wait, partitioning—that’s where we break the data into smaller chunks, right? Like dividing a pie into slices?”

Emily smiled, “More or less. Partitioning splits large tables into smaller, more manageable pieces. That way, the system doesn’t have to go through the entire dataset for every query. It’s especially useful for huge datasets like ours."

Ethan took over, gesturing toward the whiteboard. "Picture it like this. Right now, when we query the system, it's like searching an entire city for a single address. Partitioning is like dividing the city into neighborhoods. You narrow the search area from the start."

Mark uncrossed his arms, but the skepticism was still there. "And this won't affect our day- to-day operations?"

"That's where query optimization comes in," Ethan explained, drawing diagrams on the board. "We rewrite some of the most frequently used queries to take advantage of the indexes and partitions. It's about making the code as efficient as possible. Think of it like streamlining traffic on a highway—less congestion means faster results."

Jake scribbled furiously in his notebook, nodding as if everything Ethan said was gospel. "So, indexing, partitioning, and query optimization—it's like the holy trinity of SQL Server performance."

Ethan grinned. "Exactly. And all of it can be done without major disruptions. We'll monitor the impact in real-time and adjust as needed."

Mark was still cautious, but Ethan could see the wheels turning in his head. "Alright," Mark said slowly. "But how do we know these changes won't cause more problems? Downtime during peak traffic could be disastrous."

Emily stepped in. "That's why we'll test everything in a staging environment before pushing it live. We'll simulate the peak traffic, monitor performance, and make adjustments as necessary."

Ethan added, "We're also going to set up monitoring tools to track the performance of each change. Think of it like a fitness tracker for the system. If something starts to dip, we'll catch it before it spirals."

The room fell quiet for a moment, the weight of the discussion sinking in. This wasn't just about fixing the current problem. It was about setting the company up for long-term success—future-proofing their infrastructure against the inevitable data deluge.

Mark finally nodded. "Alright. Let's give it a shot."

The tension eased as they shifted the conversation to timelines and responsibilities. Jake was practically bouncing in his seat, excited to dive into the technical details. Emily, though exhausted, looked a bit more relaxed knowing there was a plan in place. Mark, ever the realist, wasn't fully convinced but was at least willing to move forward.

Later that night, Ethan found himself sitting at the kitchen table with Sarah, going over the day in his head. "You know, sometimes I wonder if we're chasing perfection," he said, leaning back in his chair.

Sarah, ever the voice of reason, smiled softly. "Perfection's a moving target. What's perfect today won't be perfect tomorrow. You just need to find the balance between getting it right and getting it done."

Ethan nodded, her words settling in. He knew she was right. The pursuit of optimization was never-ending, but at some point, you had to call it good enough and move forward.

As he headed to bed that night, the conversation with Sarah echoed in his mind. Tomorrow would bring new challenges, new data spikes, and more questions about how far they should go in their quest for optimization. But for now, he felt a sense of calm. They had a plan, and that was more than half the battle.

With a grin, Ethan thought to himself, "Optimization may not be perfection, but it's pretty damn close."

And so, with the roadmap set and the team aligned, the next phase awaited — a dive deeper into the heart of the data, where every byte counted and every query had the power to change the game.

CHAPTER V

The Heart of the Modern Data Strategy

The team had barely caught their breath from the intense discussions, when Ethan gathered everyone again to embark on the next critical phase - Integrating a Data Lake into their data architecture.

The room was a hive of activity as team members shuffled papers and prepped their notes. Ethan knew that the upcoming steps would be just as crucial as the performance optimizations they had worked so hard on.

Ethan leaned against the conference room's sleek glass table, his gaze steady and reassuring. "Alright, let's talk about Data Lakes. We've optimized our SQL Server and tackled performance bottlenecks, but now we need to think bigger. Our goal is to integrate AWS Data Lake to handle and process unstructured data."

Emily, always analytical, raised her hand. "I understand the concept, but how does a Data Lake differ from our current data storage systems? How does it handle unstructured data?"

Ethan nodded, appreciating the question. "Good question, Emily. A Data Lake is like a massive, flexible pool where we can store all kinds of data — structured data like tables and rows, and unstructured data like emails or social media posts. Unlike traditional databases, where you need to define the schema before storing data, a Data Lake allows us to store raw data and decide how to organize it later. This flexibility is crucial for integrating live data streams and making sense of diverse data types."

Jake, eager to dive into the technical details, asked, "So, what does the implementation process look like? How do we actually set up a Data Lake?"

Ethan grinned, sensing Jake's enthusiasm. "Here's a step-by-step guide. First, we'll start by setting up our AWS Data Lake environment. AWS provides tools like AWS Glue for data cataloging and AWS S3 for data storage. The process begins with data ingestion, where we collect and store data from various sources. We'll use AWS Glue to catalog and organize this data."

He continued, "Next, we need to ensure our data processing pipelines are robust. We'll use AWS Lambda functions to trigger data transformations and AWS Redshift for analytics. Essentially, we're creating a seamless flow from data collection to analysis."

Emily interjected with a thoughtful expression, "And what about data security and access control?"

Ethan replied, "Excellent point. AWS provides comprehensive security features. We'll implement encryption at rest and in transit using AWS KMS and manage access with AWS IAM roles to ensure that only authorized personnel can access the data."

Mark, skeptical but intrigued, spoke up. "I'm still concerned about the cost. Setting up and maintaining a Data Lake sounds expensive. What's the benefit compared to traditional systems?"

Ethan understood the concern and addressed it directly. "That's a valid question, Mark. While there are initial setup costs, the long-term benefits include scalability and flexibility. As our data grows, a Data Lake scales with it. Plus, it reduces the complexity of managing various data sources and formats. In the end, it's about future-proofing our data strategy."

Jake, catching the enthusiasm, added, "So, if we implement this well, we could handle massive amounts of data seamlessly. What's the next step in the implementation?"

Ethan's eyes sparkled with excitement. "The next step is to write the integration scripts. We'll use Python to automate data ingestion and transformation processes. I'll provide some code examples to get us started. For instance, here's a script that ingests data from an S3 bucket and prepares it for analysis."

As Ethan outlined the code, the team followed closely, making notes and asking questions. The script was straightforward but powerful, designed to efficiently handle large datasets and integrate them into the Data Lake.

After the meeting, Ethan sat at his desk, reflecting on the day's discussions. The integration of the Data Lake was a significant step forward, but he knew it came with its own set of challenges. He turned to Sarah, who was sitting nearby, working on her own tasks.

"So, how did the meeting go?" Sarah asked, looking up with a smile.

Ethan sighed, "It was intense but productive. We've got a clear path forward, but there's a lot of work ahead. It's like we're setting up the foundation for a huge, dynamic system."

Sarah nodded understandingly. "I'm sure you'll manage. You've tackled tough problems before."

Ethan chuckled, "Thanks. I just hope we can keep up the momentum. The Data Lake is the heart of our modern strategy, but it's only the beginning."

As Ethan looked out the window, he felt a renewed sense of purpose. The road ahead was challenging, but with the right approach, they were on their way to transforming their data strategy for the better.

The next day was a day of discussion! That morning, Ethan arrived at the office early, his mind buzzing with the ideas and insights from yesterday's meeting. The soft glow of the morning sun filtered through the windows, casting a warm light on the sleek conference room table where he'd set up for the day's brainstorming session. He arranged the whiteboard and laid out the colorful sticky notes, each one a prompt for the conversations he hoped would ignite creativity within his team.

As he brewed a fresh pot of coffee, Ethan felt a mixture of excitement and determination; today was the day they would tackle the challenges ahead and solidify their strategy around AWS Data Lake, paving the way for innovation and growth.

Ethan sat at the head of the table, sipping his coffee as the team gathered for their morning meeting. Today's topic was a heavy one, but essential for the company's next big move: managing terabyte-scale data. The challenges were real, but so were the opportunities, and Ethan was ready to dive into the nuts and bolts of how AWS Data Lake could revolutionize the way they handled and processed data.

"Alright, team," Ethan began, leaning forward, "we've been working with AWS for a while now, but managing data at this scale brings a whole new set of challenges and possibilities. Let's talk about how we're going to harness AWS Data Lake to not just cope, but thrive in this space."

Jake, always quick with a quip, chimed in, "So, basically, you're saying we're about to swim in the data ocean, but AWS Data Lake's gonna keep us from drowning?"

Ethan chuckled, "Exactly. Think of it like a data lifeboat that grows with you. The bigger the waves, the bigger the boat. Now, let's break this down through some real-world examples."

"The first case I want to discuss," Ethan continued, "involves a massive retail chain that was struggling with fragmented data coming from thousands of stores, their e-commerce platform, and customer loyalty programs. They were drowning in terabytes of structured and unstructured data, making it impossible to get a holistic view of their customers."

Ethan pulled up a slide showing the retail company's old system, a messy tangle of legacy databases and third-party platforms. "They needed a solution that could consolidate everything—from transaction data to social media interactions—into one centralized system. Enter AWS Data Lake."

Jake raised an eyebrow, "So, how did AWS Data Lake save the day?"

"Well," Ethan replied, "the company used Amazon S3 to store their vast datasets, ranging from inventory logs to real-time customer interactions. With AWS Glue, they were able to catalog and prepare this data for processing, enabling them to organize it in a way that made sense across the organization."

He paused for a moment to let the team digest this. "The real game-changer was the ability to query this raw data using Amazon Athena. The retail company could run SQL queries directly on the data in S3 without having to move it into a database, which saved them a ton of time and money. Not to mention, they could now analyze customer behavior in real time, allowing them to personalize offers, optimize inventory, and make smarter decisions."

Emily nodded thoughtfully. "And I assume the scalability was key here? Their data volumes must have grown exponentially with all those customer touchpoints."

"Exactly," Ethan confirmed. "AWS Data Lake gave them the flexibility to scale effortlessly. Their infrastructure grows with their data, without a hitch."

Next, Ethan brought up the second case study: "This one's a bit different. A major financial institution was facing challenges not only with storing terabytes of data but also with maintaining compliance and security in a cloud environment."

Jake leaned in, intrigued. "Finance, huh? So, it wasn't just about handling the data—it was about handling it securely."

"Spot on," Ethan agreed. "In the finance world, data security and regulatory compliance are paramount. This institution had years' worth of transaction logs, credit histories, and client profiles that needed to be securely stored and processed. They used AWS Data Lake as the backbone of their data architecture, but the real value came from AWS's robust security features."

He clicked to the next slide, showing how the bank employed AWS Identity and Access Management (IAM) to control who had access to sensitive data, ensuring that only authorized personnel could view or process specific datasets. Encryption at rest and in transit was also critical, with all data in Amazon S3 being encrypted using AWS Key Management Service (KMS).

"The finance team also leveraged AWS CloudTrail and Amazon Macie to monitor data access patterns and detect any suspicious activities. It was a seamless integration of security, compliance, and data processing, all within the AWS ecosystem."

Sarah, who had been quiet so far, spoke up. "So, not only did they manage to handle terabytes of data, but they also kept it safe and compliant with regulations. That's pretty powerful."

Ethan smiled. "Exactly. And by doing so, they were able to focus on their core business— delivering financial services—without worrying about the technical complexities of managing large-scale data securely."

Ethan moved on to the final example. "Let's look at healthcare. A large hospital network was generating massive amounts of data from electronic health records (EHR), medical imaging, and IoT devices like heart rate monitors and ventilators. They needed a solution that could not only store all this data but also enable real-time analytics to improve patient care."

Emily's eyes lit up. "Let me guess, AWS Data Lake?"

"You got it," Ethan replied. "They used AWS Data Lake to consolidate all patient data into a single, centralized repository. But here's where it gets interesting. They integrated machine learning models using Amazon SageMaker to predict patient outcomes based on the data collected. This allowed them to proactively intervene in high-risk cases, improving patient care and reducing costs."

He paused for emphasis. "With AWS Lambda, they were able to trigger real-time alerts for doctors and nurses whenever a patient's vitals spiked or dropped below a certain threshold.

The entire ecosystem—data collection, storage, analysis, and response—was automated and scalable."

Jake leaned back, impressed. "Man, that's next-level stuff. From retail to finance to healthcare, AWS Data Lake seems to be the Swiss Army knife for data management."

The Takeaway: AWS Data Lake as the Backbone of Data Strategy

Ethan nodded, wrapping up. "That's the beauty of AWS Data Lake—it's versatile, scalable, and secure. Whether you're dealing with terabytes of customer data, financial records, or medical information, AWS has the tools to help you manage it efficiently."

He glanced around the room, noting the thoughtful expressions on his team's faces. "Now, the question is—how do we apply these lessons to our own projects?"

With that, the team dove into a spirited discussion, brainstorming how they could leverage AWS Data Lake for their current and future data challenges. The possibilities seemed endless, but one thing was clear: AWS Data Lake would be at the heart of their data strategy.

Jake, always ready with a final word, leaned back and said with a grin, "Looks like we're diving headfirst into the Data Lake, and you know what? I think we'll swim just fine."

The room filled with laughter, the team buoyed by the possibilities ahead. As Ethan looked around, he couldn't help but smile at the camaraderie that had developed among them. Jake, with his usual enthusiasm, had just cracked a joke about their data becoming "so big it could run for president," eliciting chuckles from Emily and Mark. The light-hearted banter created an electric atmosphere, making the challenges they faced seem less daunting and more like exciting puzzles waiting to be solved.

The laughter wasn't just a distraction; it was a bonding moment that solidified their collective determination. Emily chimed in, adding her own playful quip about needing to "hire a data therapist" for their increasingly complex systems, which only prompted more jokes about their data being "emotionally unstable." This joviality allowed them to connect on a personal level, reinforcing their shared vision of navigating the intricacies of AWS Data Lake and emerging victorious.

As the laughter subsided, Ethan felt a wave of optimism wash over the team. They were not just colleagues; they were collaborators ready to dive into the deep end of data management together. This sense of unity and shared purpose made it clear that no matter what challenges lay ahead, they would tackle them as a team—full of ideas, creativity, and a little humor to keep the mood light.

CHAPTER VI

Bridging the Old and the New

The faint hum of the office's air conditioning was the only sound as Ethan sat alone, staring at the skyline through his large office window. His desk was scattered with notes, diagrams, and sticky reminders of the steps his team needed to take next. The glow of his monitor bathed the room in a cool light, mirroring the intensity of his thoughts.

He leaned back in his chair, tapping his pen against the edge of the table as he reflected on how far they'd come. They had tackled scalability and optimization, but now it was time to bring everything together—to bridge the gap between their legacy systems and the new tools that would take them into the future.

Ethan's mind wandered for a moment, flashing back to when he first started with the company.

Back then, their data infrastructure had been simple. They had a single SQL Server instance, and everything worked like a charm — until the customer base exploded and the data grew faster than anyone had anticipated. "It's funny," Ethan thought to himself, "how something that once felt so cutting-edge now feels ancient."

Today, they were integrating AWS Data Lake with SQL Server, along with machine learning models and business intelligence (BI) tools. It felt like trying to make a smartphone work with an old rotary phone.

The door creaked open, breaking his thoughts, and Emily and Jake walked in, both juggling laptops and coffee mugs.

"Morning, boss. Ready for another round of digital wizardry?" Jake said with a grin, setting his mug down on the table with a dramatic flourish.

Ethan chuckled. "More like making sure the magic doesn't turn into a disaster. You've got your cape on, right?"

Emily rolled her eyes but smiled. "You two are ridiculous. But yes, we're here for the fun stuff—tool integration day! Or as I like to call it, 'Let's not break anything important.'"

The mood was light, but Ethan knew the task ahead was a serious one. "Alright, team," he said, straightening up. "We've optimized, we've scaled, and now we need to integrate everything. SQL Server, AWS Data Lake, our ETL processes, machine learning models, and BI tools. This is where it all comes together."

Jake was the first to speak up, his excitement palpable. "So, how do we start integrating SQL Server with AWS Data Lake? I know they're fundamentally different in how they store and manage data."

Ethan nodded. "Great question. So, here's the thing — SQL Server is all about structured data. Rows, columns, tables, you know the drill.

AWS Data Lake, on the other hand, is more like a giant swimming pool where you can throw in anything — structured data, unstructured data, semi-structured data, you name it. Our challenge is to create a bridge between the two so that data can flow back and forth seamlessly."

Emily chimed in, her voice calm and measured. "That's where ETL—Extract, Transform, Load—comes in. We need to extract the data from SQL Server, transform it into a format that AWS Data Lake can understand, and load it into the Data Lake. But it's not just about moving data. We need to ensure that both systems can work together, continuously exchanging data without losing any information."

Jake rubbed his chin thoughtfully. "And we'll also need to make sure the BI tools can pull data from both places, right? We don't want our dashboards to suddenly go blank just because the data is sitting in two different systems."

"Exactly," Ethan said. "We'll use AWS Glue to catalog the data in the Data Lake, making it searchable and accessible. Once that's done, we can connect our BI tools to AWS Athena, which allows us to query the Data Lake using SQL."

Jake smirked. "So it's like trying to teach an old dog new tricks—only the dog is our SQL Server, and the tricks are cross-system queries."

Emily laughed. "Pretty much. Just make sure the dog doesn't forget how to sit while learning how to roll over."

Once they had mapped out the integration steps, Ethan leaned forward, a spark of excitement dancing in his eyes. His voice took on a new energy as he spoke. "Alright, let's take this up a notch. We've been focusing on integrating SQL Server and AWS Data Lake, but why stop there? Let's throw in some predictive power — integrate a machine learning model to predict customer churn."

Jake practically jumped out of his seat, his excitement bubbling over like a kid who just got the golden ticket. His energy was contagious, lighting up the room as he leaned forward, eyes wide, hands gesturing animatedly. "This is exactly what I've been waiting for!" he exclaimed, his voice a little louder than intended.

His enthusiasm was so palpable it was almost as if the air around him crackled with it. He couldn't sit still, shifting in his chair, practically bouncing on the balls of his feet. "Machine learning models, real-time data integration—this is the cool stuff! I mean, come on! We're not just keeping up with the future, we're shaping it! How awesome is that?" His eyes darted to Ethan, then Emily, as if waiting for confirmation that they, too, felt the electricity in the air.

Ethan, watching Jake's exuberance, couldn't help but grin. This was why he loved having Jake on the team—the guy was like a human spark plug.

"Ooooh, machine learning! This is where the real fun begins. So, we'll use the historical customer data from SQL Server, right?" His fingers hovered above his laptop, eager to dive in.

Ethan nodded, his smile widening. "Exactly. We'll extract that data and push it into the Data Lake.

Once it's there, we can harness the power of *SageMaker*—AWS's machine learning platform—to build, train, and deploy a model that can predict which customers are likely to leave us."

Emily, always the practical one, leaned back in her chair, arms crossed as she raised an eyebrow. "And let me guess—we're not just going to run the model in isolation. We're going to integrate it back into our live data flow so it can actually provide real-time insights, right?"

Ethan grinned, loving how Emily could always cut straight to the heart of the matter. "Exactly. We'll set it up so that the model pulls new customer data in real-time, from both SQL Server and AWS Data Lake. Every time new data is fed into the system, the model will make fresh predictions.

And here's the kicker! We'll automate it using AWS Lambda functions so it runs without us having to babysit it."

Jake's eyes gleamed with mischief. "So basically, we're building a robot fortune teller that can predict which customers are going to ghost us."

Ethan laughed. "Well, I like to think of it as 'intelligent automation,' but sure, we can call it a fortune teller if it makes you happy."

Emily wasn't quite done with her questions though. "Hold on, won't we need to clean up and prep the data first before feeding it to the model? I mean, we're dealing with structured data in SQL, and the Data Lake probably has some messy unstructured stuff in there too."

Ethan leaned back, appreciating how sharp his team was. "Good point. We'll use AWS Glue to catalog and transform the data in the Data Lake. That'll help clean up any inconsistencies and make sure everything's ready for the model to ingest. We're not just dumping raw data into the model—it needs to be prepped, transformed, and formatted just right."

Jake clapped his hands together. "Perfect! So, SageMaker will do the heavy lifting on the training side. We feed it the data, tune the parameters, and it spits out the churn predictions. Then Lambda functions swoop in to automate it all, and BAM—real-time predictions, all day, every day."

Ethan couldn't help but chuckle. Jake always had a way of making things sound more dramatic than they were, but he was right. This was the kind of integration that would move the needle. The ability to predict customer churn before it happened was a game-changer, giving their team an edge in customer retention.

Emily, never one to get swept away by excitement without double-checking, raised her hand slightly. "What about edge cases? I mean, what happens if the model starts giving us skewed predictions or if the data stream gets interrupted? We're going to need some kind of monitoring in place, right?"

"Always the realist," Ethan said, shaking his head with a grin. "Yes, we'll definitely need monitoring. We'll use Amazon CloudWatch to track the performance of the Lambda functions and monitor the predictions the model churns out. If anything goes off track, we'll be alerted immediately. It's like having guardrails in place to keep everything running smoothly."

Jake leaned back in his chair, folding his arms behind his head. "You know, this is starting to sound like the perfect blend of cutting-edge tech and hands-off automation. We'll build the system, and then it'll basically take care of itself."

Ethan shook his head, smirking. "Nice try, Jake. Systems like this always need fine-tuning. We'll be iterating on the model, tweaking the parameters, and keeping an eye on the data quality. No fortune teller is perfect."

Jake sighed dramatically. "So much for the 'hands-off' dream."

Emily, enjoying Jake's playful disappointment, leaned over and patted him on the shoulder. "Welcome to the reality of machine learning. It's not magic—just really smart math."

Ethan chuckled, the mood light but the task ahead serious. This wasn't just about integrating SQL Server and AWS Data Lake; they were taking it a step further by layering machine learning on top of their unified data architecture. The goal wasn't just to store data efficiently—it was to use it to gain actionable insights, real-time predictions, and ultimately make smarter business decisions.

The room buzzed with a sense of momentum as they prepared to dig into the next phase of their work. The machine learning integration was going to be a challenge, but the payoff? Huge.

As Ethan watched Emily and Jake dive into the code, collaborating and bouncing ideas off each other, he couldn't help but feel a surge of pride. They were building something remarkable here—bridging the old and the new, structured and unstructured data, human intelligence and machine learning. It was the kind of work that kept him going, no matter how complex it got.

And at the end of the day, if they could predict customer churn before it happened, well...maybe Jake was right.

They were building a kind of digital fortune teller after all.

As Ethan closed his laptop, a faint smile tugged at the corners of his mouth, but his mind was already wandering. They had managed to bridge the old systems with new technologies, creating a hybrid solution that was as seamless as it was powerful. But something gnawed at him. Data wasn't just growing—it was evolving, mutating, shifting in ways that no one could predict. Every time they conquered one challenge, the next one seemed even more complex.

He leaned back in his chair, glancing out the window as twilight settled over the city. The glow of streetlights flickered on, mirroring the constant hum of technology that never slept. In the world of data, evolution was relentless. Would they be ready for what came next?

He wasn't entirely sure, but one thing he knew for certain: whatever it was, they'd face it together. His team was too sharp, too driven, and—let's be real—too stubborn to let anything beat them.

Just as his thoughts were winding down, Jake burst back into the room with his signature flair. "So, what's next, Captain? We going to teach the robots to make us coffee now?"

Emily, without missing a beat, chimed in. "Oh please, if we leave it up to you, the robots would end up brewing energy drinks mixed with pizza sauce."

Jake raised his hands in mock defence. "Hey, who says that's a bad thing? I'm just trying to think outside the box."

Ethan grinned, leaning into the banter. "If by 'outside the box,' you mean food poisoning, then yeah, you've got that nailed."

Emily snickered. "Or maybe we could build a machine learning model to predict Jake's next terrible idea before he even speaks."

Jake gasped dramatically. "Excuse me, I'm an innovator! My ideas aren't terrible—they're ahead of their time."

"Way ahead," Ethan said with a laugh. "So far ahead that civilization hasn't even invented the facepalm strong enough for them."

Jake crossed his arms, pouting like a kid denied a cookie. "One day, you'll all see. My pizza- energy drink hybrid will take the world by storm."

Emily shook her head, smiling. "And that, Jake, is how you end up on the 'Do Not Hire' list for every future company."

The laughter faded as they settled into a more reflective mood, the weight of the day's achievements sinking in. Ethan's gaze drifted back to his laptop, now closed but still humming in his mind.

"Seriously though," Jake said, a bit more grounded, "what's the next mountain to climb?"

Ethan paused, his hand resting on the edge of the table, his eyes narrowing as his thoughts spiraled deeper into the problem. He scanned the room, feeling the weight of the moment. The hum of the office was faint in the background, almost drowned out by the intensity of his own thoughts. "The thing is," he began, his voice slow and deliberate, "we've bridged the old systems with the new, but it's never really over, is it?"

He glanced at Emily, Jake, and Mark, who were watching him intently. The light from the monitors cast a soft glow across their faces, but the atmosphere was anything but soft. Ethan's mind raced through the implications of what they had accomplished. Sure, they had managed to integrate the legacy systems with AWS Data Lake, tackled machine learning models, and automated processes that once seemed untouchable. But deep down, he knew this wasn't the finish line—it was just a pit stop.

"Technology keeps moving, evolving," Ethan continued, his voice gaining momentum as he articulated the challenge that kept gnawing at him. "Every time we fix something or integrate a new tool, the next advancement is already on the horizon. Today, it's machine learning models predicting customer churn; tomorrow, it's something else entirely. Quantum computing, AI-driven data governance, who knows?"

He ran a hand through his hair, the slight tension in his jaw visible as he spoke. "We can't just build and sit back, thinking we're done. We have to evolve with it—constantly." There was a sense of urgency now, not panic, but the realization that their work was part of a never-ending cycle. Every solution, every innovation, was just one step toward the next wave of technology that would inevitably disrupt their systems again.

The silence in the room was thick with understanding. Emily nodded, her arms crossed, looking contemplative. Jake's usual joking demeanor had been replaced with a rare, serious expression. They all knew the truth behind Ethan's words. It wasn't just about staying current—it was about anticipating the future, about being proactive instead of reactive.

"And that's the real challenge," Ethan added, his eyes meeting each of theirs. "Not just solving today's problems, but preparing for the ones we can't even see coming."

Jake quipped, "So basically, you're saying we'll never sleep again?"

Ethan chuckled. "Pretty much."

Emily leaned back in her chair, smirking. "Well, I hear coffee stocks are a good investment right now."

"Good thing Jake's working on his robot barista plan then," Ethan joked.

They shared one last laugh, but underneath it all, they knew the truth. The world of data was always changing, and they'd need to stay sharp for whatever came next. Because the thing about evolution? It never stops.

As Ethan locked eyes with his team, a final thought crossed his mind. The challenges ahead might be unpredictable, but with this group—well, they might just be ready for anything.

And the next big evolution?

They were already preparing for it.

"Alright," Ethan said, standing up, "let's get some rest before Jake actually invents something catastrophic."

Jake grinned. "Or genius."

"Let's not take any chances," Emily added with a wink.

As they headed out, Ethan felt the excitement simmering just below the surface. Tomorrow might bring another mountain, but they'd tackle it the only way they knew how—together.

And whatever came next... would be worth the climb. "Brace yourselves, the future is coming," Ethan muttered with a grin, just loud enough for them to hear.

"Bring it on," Jake shouted from the hallway.

Jake, catching Ethan's contemplative mood, concluded the chat with a grin, “Well, if technology is always changing, at least it keeps us on our toes! I guess we better start stocking up on coffee — looks like we've got a future full of sleepless nights ahead!”

Emily chuckled, adding, "And I suppose that means we'll have to keep upgrading our skills. Or we could just invent a coffee machine that writes code for us!" The room burst into laughter, the camaraderie palpable. As the team bantered and joked, Ethan couldn't shake the feeling that they were on the brink of something even bigger. "Here's to the future," he said, raising an imaginary glass, "whatever it brings, we'll face it head-on. Because that's what we do."

And with that, the team's laughter filled the room, their shared optimism a beacon guiding them toward the next great challenge. Their camaraderie and enthusiasm were palpable, a stark contrast to the stress that had once hung over their previous projects.

This renewed energy carried into their discussions as they gathered around the whiteboard. Ethan began scribbling down a comparison of the old system's costs versus the new AWS- based solution.

The old system had been a patchwork of various components — hardware, software, and maintenance contracts — all stacked up in a tangled mess of expenses.

Every month, they were hit with bills for server upkeep, software licenses, and labor costs for emergency fixes. It was a costly affair, with expenses steadily rising as the system struggled to keep pace with growing data demands.

In contrast, the new AWS-based solution offered a more streamlined and predictable cost structure. AWS's pay-as-you-go model meant that the company would only pay for the resources they actually used. No more hefty maintenance fees for underutilized servers or surprise costs for unexpected outages.

Ethan broke it down further, pointing out how AWS's scalable architecture allowed them to adjust resources based on demand, optimizing costs and reducing waste. For instance, by leveraging AWS's auto-scaling capabilities, they could handle peak traffic periods without needing to invest in expensive, high-capacity servers that sat idle during quieter times.

The discussion then shifted to the long-term financial benefits of AWS. Unlike their old system, which required frequent upgrades and replacements, AWS provided regular updates and innovations as part of its service. Ethan emphasized that this not only saved on hardware costs but also ensured they were always using the latest technology without additional investment.

Additionally, AWS's built-in security features reduced the need for costly third-party solutions, offering a more secure and cost-effective approach to data management.

Emily chimed in with a practical example, her tone both informative and reassuring. "Think of it like renting an apartment versus buying a house," she said, gesturing with her hands to emphasize her point.

"When you rent an apartment, you're not worried about the cost of repairs, property taxes, or the hassle of maintenance. You just pay your rent, and if something breaks, the landlord handles it. Now, with AWS, it's like we're renting a space that grows with us. We don't have to worry about property taxes or repairs. We just pay for what we use and enjoy the benefits of regular upgrades and scalability."

The team nodded in agreement, the analogy making the benefits of AWS crystal clear. The comparison struck a chord, highlighting that while the initial setup of AWS might seem daunting — like signing a new lease — the long-term financial advantages were substantial. The ongoing costs of their old system, with its patchwork of servers, licenses, and emergency fixes, were rapidly stacking up. In contrast, AWS offered a streamlined, cost-effective solution that would allow them to scale effortlessly as their needs evolved.

It was becoming increasingly evident that transitioning to AWS wasn't just a smart move for their technology—it was a financially savvy decision that would soon start paying dividends.

Ethan and Jake sat together at a corner table, papers and charts spread out between them. Ethan had his laptop open, showing a detailed cost analysis of the old system versus the new AWS-based solution. Jake, ever the eager learner, peered intently at the screen.

"Alright, Jake," Ethan began, pointing to the first chart. "Let's break this down. Our old system was like a Frankenstein's monster of tech. We've got hardware costs, software licenses, and a never-ending stream of maintenance bills. Every month, it was something new—server issues, software updates, you name it. The cost of keeping it all running was steadily climbing."

Jake nodded, absorbing the information. "Got it. And AWS? How does that stack up?"

Ethan switched to the AWS cost breakdown, which was much simpler. "With AWS, we pay as we go. There's no upfront investment in hardware, no expensive maintenance contracts. We pay for the storage we use, the compute power we need, and the data transfer that happens. Plus, AWS handles all the updates and scaling automatically."

Jake's eyes widened as he saw the stark difference in the numbers. "So, it's like the difference between buying a new car and leasing one. With the old system, we're stuck with a clunky, old car that needs constant repairs. With AWS, we're leasing a shiny new model with all the latest features and no maintenance headaches."

Ethan grinned, appreciating Jake's analogy. "Exactly! And, to put it in perspective, keeping the old system is like paying for a high-maintenance pet—always needing attention and eating up your budget. Switching to AWS is like having a goldfish—low maintenance and only costing you when you feed it."

Jake chuckled, "I guess I'd rather deal with a goldfish than a needy dog, especially when it comes to cost!"

Ethan laughed, "Agreed! And hopefully, AWS will be as easy to handle as a goldfish, with far fewer messes to clean up!"

As Ethan and his team wrapped up their discussion, it was clear that the integration of old and new systems was more than just a technical challenge—it was a pivotal moment for their company's future.

They had delved deep into the cost benefits of transitioning to AWS, examined the practical aspects of integrating cutting-edge tools like machine learning models, and embraced the importance of teamwork in navigating these changes. The realization that AWS offered a more cost-effective, scalable, and maintainable solution had solidified their decision to move forward with the new technology.

The air in the room buzzed with a sense of accomplishment and optimism. The team's laughter and camaraderie were a testament to their unity and shared vision.

Ethan reflected on the journey, recognizing that while the road ahead was still filled with uncertainties, they were well-equipped to face whatever came next. They had bridged the gap between old and new, not just with technology but with a renewed sense of purpose and collaboration.

As Ethan closed his notebook and looked around at his team, he couldn't help but feel a surge of excitement. "Alright, team," he said with a grin, "we've tackled the cost comparisons and integrated some amazing tech.

Now, let's get ready for the next adventure—because in the world of data, there's always another challenge waiting just around the corner."

Jake, always quick with a quip, added, "Well, if the next challenge is as fun as this one, I'm ready to dive in. Just make sure it doesn't involve any more goldfish jokes!"

The team burst into laughter, their spirits high.

As they prepared to tackle the next phase of their project, Ethan felt a deep sense of satisfaction. They were ready for whatever lay ahead, and with their combined skills and enthusiasm, they knew they could conquer any challenge the future might bring.

CHAPTER VII

Navigating Stormy Waters

The evening was settling in, and the team from Ethan's office had gathered at "The Tech Tavern," a popular bar known for its retro ambiance and quirky tech-themed décor. The bar's walls were adorned with vintage computer parts and old-school arcade games, creating a nostalgic yet modern atmosphere. Neon lights cast a soft glow over the room, and the hum of casual conversation mixed with the clinking of glasses and the occasional burst of laughter.

Ethan and his team were seated at a round table in a cozy corner of the bar, their spirits buoyed by a long week of tackling challenges. Emily was enjoying a classic burger topped with crispy bacon and cheddar, her favorite comfort food.

Jake had ordered a towering plate of nachos loaded with cheese, jalapeños, and guacamole, his enthusiasm for both the dish and the evening evident in his wide grin. Mark had opted for a hearty steak, and Emily's go-to cocktail, a perfectly mixed mojito, was making its way around the table. Ethan, ever the fan of craft beers, was sipping on a local IPA with a hoppy aroma that filled the air.

"So," Jake started, after taking a hearty bite of nacho, "we survived another week of tech madness. What's the plan for tonight? - Are we discussing the next big thing or just indulging in this amazing cheese?" He grinned, gesturing to the plate of nachos with exaggerated enthusiasm.

Ethan chuckled, "Well, Jake, as much as I'd love to dive into a cheese discussion, we've got a bit of a serious topic to cover. We've had our fair share of challenges lately, and I think it's time we get down to some real talk about how we're going to handle them."

Emily, sipping her mojito, raised an eyebrow. "Real talk? That sounds like a fancy way of saying we're about to dive into the nitty-gritty of performance bottlenecks, security issues, and cost management."

"You've got it," Ethan said, nodding. "We've been doing a lot of problem-solving lately, but I think it's important to make sure we're all on the same page about the common challenges we face and how we can tackle them."

Mark, who had been quietly enjoying his steak, leaned in. "Alright, I have a game. What's the biggest challenge we're facing right now?"

Ethan took a sip of his beer, savoring the frothy head before setting the glass down with a thoughtful clink. "Performance bottlenecks, data security, and cost management. These are the big three that have been on our radar. Each one has its own set of complications, but together, they create a perfect storm of issues that can be tough to navigate."

He leaned forward, his expression serious. "Let's break them down. First up, performance bottlenecks. Imagine you're trying to funnel a large volume of water through a narrow pipe. The pipe can only handle so much water at a time before it gets clogged. In tech terms, a performance bottleneck is like that narrow pipe — it's a part of our system that's limiting the overall performance because it can't keep up with the demands being placed on it. It might be a slow database query, a poorly optimized algorithm, or an overloaded server. Identifying and addressing these bottlenecks is crucial because if the system is slow or unresponsive, it impacts everything from user satisfaction to operational efficiency."

Emily nodded, her brow furrowed in concentration. "So, if our system is slowing down because one part of it can't handle the load, that's a bottleneck?"

"Exactly," Ethan affirmed. "Now, moving on to data security. This is all about protecting our data from unauthorized access and breaches. With sensitive information like customer details and financial records, we need robust security measures to ensure it doesn't fall into the wrong hands. This includes encryption, which is like putting our data in a locked safe that only authorized people can open. It also involves using access controls to make sure that only the right people have the right permissions to view or modify the data. Implementing tools like AWS Identity and Access Management (IAM) can help manage who gets access to what."

Jake, ever the tech enthusiast, chimed in, “And data security is critical because a breach could mean losing customer trust and facing legal consequences, right?”

“Spot on,” Ethan agreed. “Finally, we have cost management. This is about making sure we’re not spending more than we need to on our tech infrastructure. Cloud services like AWS offer flexibility and scalability, but if we’re not careful, costs can spiral out of control. We need to monitor our usage and optimize our resources to avoid unnecessary expenses. Think of it as making sure we’re not leaving the lights on in every room of a house we’re only using a few rooms in. Tools like AWS Cost Explorer can help track and manage these expenses.”

Emily laughed, “So, it’s like making sure we’re not overpaying for a gym membership we never use?”

“Exactly!” Ethan said with a grin. “In short, tackling performance bottlenecks, ensuring data security, and managing costs effectively are like juggling three flaming torches. They each require careful attention and skill. But when we handle them well, our systems run smoothly, securely, and cost-effectively.”

Jake, looking both serious and amused, added, “So, our job is to keep the torches from setting everything on fire?”

“Pretty much,” Ethan laughed. “And remember, we’ve got the right team and tools to make sure those torches stay under control.”

The team’s laughter mingled with the clinking of glasses, their camaraderie and shared understanding strengthening their resolve to tackle the challenges ahead. As they continued their discussion, it was clear that while the road ahead was fraught with obstacles, their collective expertise and teamwork would be the key to navigating the stormy waters.

Jake, never one to shy away from diving into the technical deep end, leaned forward with interest starting to deep drive in the topic - “Let’s restart with performance bottlenecks. What exactly are we looking at?”

Emily nodded. “Performance bottlenecks are those pesky issues that slow down our systems. They can be anything from inefficient queries to poorly optimized indexes. It’s like having a highway with a bunch of traffic jams.”

Ethan agreed. “Exactly. And to tackle these, we need to look at optimizing our SQL queries, implementing better indexing strategies, and considering partitioning our data to improve performance. It’s all about finding and removing the ‘traffic jams’ in our data flow.”

Jake took a sip of his drink, then added, “And then there’s data security. That’s like trying to keep a secret in a room full of gossiping friends. How do we ensure our data is safe from prying eyes?”

Ethan smiled. “Data security is indeed crucial. We need to implement strong encryption methods, set up firewalls, and regularly audit our security practices. It’s all about making sure that only the right people have access to the right information.”

Mark, who had been following the conversation closely, chimed in, “And what about cost management? That’s where things get really interesting. How do we balance our budget while still getting the most out of our technology?”

Emily responded, “Cost management is like balancing a checkbook while trying to get the best deal on a shopping spree. With AWS, for instance, we can often find cost-effective solutions that scale with our needs. We just need to be smart about how we use our resources.”

Jake, ever the jokester, grinned. “So basically, we’re trying to make sure we don’t blow our budget while still getting the tech equivalent of a shopping spree? Sounds like a high-stakes game.”

Ethan laughed. “Pretty much! The goal is to make sure we’re investing wisely and getting the best bang for our buck.”

As the evening wore on, the conversation flowed as freely as the drinks, moving seamlessly from technical talk to light-hearted banter. Ethan found himself reflecting on the team's camaraderie and the challenges they faced together. Despite the hurdles, the team's ability to approach problems with humor and creativity made every challenge seem surmountable.

"So," Ethan said with a grin, "after all this tech talk, what's our game plan for tomorrow?"

Jake, with a mischievous sparkle in his eye, replied, "Well, I think we should tackle these challenges head-on. And if we end up needing more nachos along the way, I'm definitely not opposed!"

The team erupted in laughter, their spirits high and their resolve strengthened. As they finished their meals and prepared to head out, Ethan felt a renewed sense of optimism. The road ahead was bound to be challenging, but with this team, he was confident they could navigate any stormy waters that came their way.

Ethan leaned back in his chair, his eyes reflecting the warm glow of the bar's neon lights. "Before we call it a night, let me share a real-world example of how a major financial institution tackled security challenges in a cloud environment. It's a story that might give us a bit more perspective on our own journey."

The team, intrigued, settled back into their seats, eager to hear more.

"A few years ago," Ethan began, "a large financial institution faced a significant security breach. They had recently migrated their operations to the cloud, and while the transition promised greater flexibility and scalability, it also introduced new security challenges. The institution had to deal with a breach that exposed sensitive customer data. The incident was a wake-up call for them."

Emily raised an eyebrow. "That sounds intense. How did they handle it?"

Ethan nodded. "They approached it with a multi-faceted strategy. First, they implemented stringent encryption protocols for data at rest and in transit. They used AWS Key Management Service (KMS) for managing their encryption keys, ensuring that all data was securely encrypted. They also set up AWS Identity and Access Management (IAM) to enforce strict access controls and ensure that only authorized personnel could access sensitive information."

Jake, always quick to pick up on the technical details, asked, "So they basically locked everything up tight and made sure only the right people had the right keys?"

"Exactly," Ethan said. "They also employed AWS CloudTrail and AWS Config to continuously monitor and audit their cloud resources. This helped them keep an eye on any suspicious activities and quickly address potential vulnerabilities. Additionally, they engaged in regular security assessments and penetration testing to identify and fix any weaknesses before they could be exploited."

Mark, impressed, commented, "That sounds like a well-rounded approach. They didn't just fix the problem; they proactively strengthened their defenses."

Ethan grinned. "Absolutely. The key takeaway from their experience is that security in the cloud isn't a one-time fix but an ongoing commitment. It requires constant vigilance and adaptation to new threats."

Emily, always the practical one, nodded thoughtfully. "So, our focus should be on integrating strong security measures from the start and continuously monitoring for any potential issues."

Ethan agreed. "Exactly. Just like the financial institution, we need to ensure our systems are secure and resilient. And remember, as we face our own challenges, we can take comfort in knowing that we're not alone in this journey. Many organizations have navigated similar waters and come out stronger on the other side."

Jake, with a twinkle in his eye, added, "And if we ever need a break from the serious stuff, we've got nachos and laughs to keep us going!"

The team laughed, their camaraderie strengthening with each shared moment. As they prepared to leave the bar, Ethan felt a renewed sense of confidence and purpose. The challenges ahead were significant, but with this team by his side, he was ready to face them head-on.

The evening's conversation had not only reinforced their strategies but also highlighted the importance of teamwork and continuous improvement. As they clinked their glasses in a final toast, Ethan knew that no matter how stormy the waters ahead, they were well-equipped to navigate them together.

With a final chuckle, Ethan said, "To tackling challenges, learning from real-world examples, and making sure our journey is as smooth as possible — one nacho at a time!"

And as the team exited The Tech Tavern, their laughter and optimism echoed through the night, a reminder that no challenge was too great when faced with determination, teamwork, and a touch of humor.

CHAPTER VIII

Sailing into the Future

The sky was a deep shade of violet as Ethan stepped onto the rooftop of Skyline Retreat, one of the trendiest spots in the city. Fairy lights lined the wooden decking, casting a soft glow over tables filled with murmuring conversations.

Ethan's team was gathered around a large table near the edge, the city sprawling below them. Tonight's discussion wasn't about immediate tasks or looming deadlines — it was about the future.

Jake took a long sip from his beer, relishing the hoppy flavor before leaning back in his chair, a mischievous grin dancing on his lips. He scanned the room, noting the relaxed atmosphere— the dim lights, soft chatter of patrons mingling around, and the faint hum of music filtering in from the speakers. Breaking the ice, he casually tossed out, "So, what's the buzzword for next year? AI? Machine learning? Or are we talking about quantum computing now?"

The table erupted in laughter, the levity of the moment washing over them. Emily raised an eyebrow, a playful challenge in her gaze. "Quantum computing? Jake, I think you're just trying to sound smart. You can't even program a coffee machine without it spitting out cold brew instead of espresso!"

Mark chuckled, nodding. "Yeah, and besides, AI and machine learning are already on everyone's lips. Quantum computing sounds like something out of a sci-fi movie. We need to keep it real here—like, can our data even handle that level of complexity?"

Jake shrugged, undeterred. "Hey, if we're going to dream, let's dream big! But seriously, AI and machine learning are where it's at right now. Imagine algorithms that learn from data patterns, helping us predict customer behavior and automate decision-making processes. It's like giving our data a brain!"

Ethan chimed in, intrigued. “Exactly! The real game-changer is how we harness these technologies to enhance our data strategies. It’s not just about throwing AI at a problem; it’s about integrating it thoughtfully into our workflows. We need to be strategic about it.”

“True,” Emily agreed, swirling her drink thoughtfully. “But let’s not forget the importance of ethics in AI. We’re dealing with data that affects real lives. If we’re not careful, we could end up creating biases instead of solutions.”

Jake laughed, raising his glass. “Well, at least if we mess up, we’ll have plenty of ‘data’ to explain ourselves! Just remember, if the robots take over, I’m not going down without a fight!”

Ethan smiled, setting down his glass of bourbon. “It’s all of the above. Data management is changing faster than we can keep up with. AI and machine learning are just the start. The real challenge is figuring out how to implement them at scale, integrate them with our current systems, and make them work for us without breaking the bank.”

Emily chimed in, pushing her glasses up her nose. “But how do we stay ahead of the curve? I mean, look at how fast things have evolved. Ten years ago, we were just starting to talk about cloud storage, and now we’re processing terabytes in real-time across multiple platforms.”

Ethan nodded. “That’s exactly the point. AI and machine learning are more than just trends— they’re the future of data processing. But they come with challenges. Take machine learning models for example. Sure, we can use them to predict customer behavior or identify patterns in real-time, but the data has to be clean, well-structured, and the algorithms trained properly. We’ll need to invest in not just the tools, but also the people who can make sense of it all.”

Jake leaned forward, grinning. “Basically, we’re talking about hiring a bunch of data ninjas.”

Emily laughed. “Or at least training the team we have to become data ninjas. We can't just rely on the tech alone; we need people who can think creatively and solve problems."

The conversation buzzed with excitement as they dove into the implications of AI, machine learning, and the potential for automating complex workflows. Ethan listened to the ideas flowing around the table, feeling a mixture of excitement and apprehension. They were sailing into uncharted waters, but they were doing it together.

Later that night, Ethan found himself sitting at another rooftop bar, this time with just Sarah. The view was just as breathtaking, the lights of the city twinkling in the distance, but the conversation had shifted. It was quieter, more reflective. The faint hum of traffic below was the only interruption to the stillness.

Sarah took a sip from her glass of white wine and leaned forward, resting her chin on her hand. "You seemed deep in thought tonight. What's going on in that brain of yours?"

Ethan chuckled softly, stirring the ice in his whiskey. "It's just... the future of everything. AI, machine learning, data lakes... It's all moving so fast. We're talking about systems that can predict customer behavior before they even know what they want. It's exciting but also overwhelming."

Sarah tilted her head, her eyes searching his. "And you're worried about staying relevant?"

He nodded slowly. "Yeah. I mean, it's one thing to know the technology, but it's another to evolve with it. The world is changing, and the industry is always looking for the next big thing. I want to be ahead of that curve, not trailing behind it. But sometimes, I wonder if I'll be able to keep up."

Sarah smiled, reaching across the table to squeeze his hand. "You've always been ahead of the game, Ethan. The fact that you're even thinking about this shows you're already adapting. And besides, you've got your team. You don't have to figure it all out on your own."

Ethan sighed, taking in her words as the cool night air brushed his face.

"You're right. It's just... I feel like we're on the edge of something big, and I don't want to miss the wave."

She laughed, her eyes sparkling in the moonlight. "You're not going to miss it. You'll be riding it, probably with some fancy AI surfboard."

He grinned, the tension easing from his shoulders. "Fancy AI surfboard, huh? Now that's a trend I could get behind."

The conversation turned lighter after that, but Ethan couldn't help but reflect on the deeper issues. Technology was evolving at lightning speed, and with it, the expectations of people in the industry. But Sarah was right. He didn't have to do it alone. With his team by his side and a willingness to adapt, Ethan felt more ready than ever to sail into the future.

The next morning, back at the office, Ethan called for a leadership meeting. As they sat around the conference table, he began, "It's time we seriously consider investing in AI-driven data analytics. The landscape is shifting, and we need to move with it if we want to stay ahead. AI isn't just a tool for the future—it's our next step."

Ethan stood at the head of the conference table, the morning light filtering through the large windows behind him. He knew this was an important meeting—not just for him, but for the entire company. The shift they were about to make would determine how they positioned themselves in the rapidly evolving landscape of data management.

"AI-driven data analytics," Ethan began, "isn't just a buzzword anymore. It's the next logical step in our journey to stay ahead of the curve. We've spent the last few years building robust systems to process and manage terabytes of data. But managing data is only part of the battle. Now, we need to get smarter with it. We need to extract more value from our data, and that's where AI comes in."

He paused for a moment, watching the expressions around the table. Some team members, like Emily, were already nodding in agreement, but others, like Jake, looked intrigued but hesitant.

Ethan continued, "AI-driven data analytics allows us to go beyond just storing and processing data. It gives us the power to analyze patterns, predict trends, and make decisions in real time. Imagine being able to anticipate customer needs before they even know what they want, or identifying operational inefficiencies before they cause a problem. That's what AI can do for us. It's not just reactive—it's proactive."

Jake leaned forward, curiosity piqued. "Okay, but what does that actually look like for us? We've got mountains of data. How does AI help us sift through it all?"

Ethan smiled, glad Jake asked the question. "Great point, Jake. Think of it like this—AI doesn't just process data faster. It learns from it. It identifies patterns, relationships, and anomalies that would take humans months, if not years, to recognize. Take customer behavior, for example. AI can analyze past transactions, website clicks, social media engagement, and even weather patterns to predict what a customer might want to buy next. But it doesn't stop there. The AI models get smarter the more data they process, refining their predictions with each new piece of information."

Emily chimed in, her excitement evident. "It's like giving our data a brain! The more we feed it, the better it gets at figuring out the important stuff."

Ethan nodded. "Exactly. And it's not just about predictions. AI can help with operational efficiency too. Think about optimizing supply chains, predicting equipment failure, or automating decision-making processes. Instead of manually analyzing spreadsheets, AI can do the heavy lifting, allowing us to focus on strategy and innovation. It's like upgrading our toolset from a hammer to a precision laser."

The team was beginning to warm up to the idea. Ethan knew the leap from traditional data analytics to AI-driven systems could seem daunting, but the potential was too big to ignore.

"But," Ethan said, leaning against the table, "it's not without its challenges. Implementing AI requires more than just technology. It's about mindset. We need people who can not only understand the data but also build the models and systems to make sense of it. That means investing in the right talent and infrastructure to support this shift."

Jake raised his hand, jokingly. "So... we're basically going to become a team of data ninjas?" The room erupted in laughter, and Ethan grinned. "Something like that, yeah. But seriously,

this is going to require us to think differently about how we approach data. AI-driven analytics will allow us to be more agile and responsive, but it also means we have to be open to new ways of working."

Ethan walked to the whiteboard and started sketching out a simple diagram. "Let's take a real-world example. A major financial institution recently faced massive data security concerns when they moved their operations to the cloud. They were handling sensitive customer information and needed to ensure that the data not only remained secure but also accessible in real-time. Using AI-driven data analytics, they were able to build a system that continuously monitored their data for potential breaches, alerting the team to any anomalies. Over time, the AI model learned the patterns of regular activity and could identify outliers, preventing potential attacks before they could even happen."

The team's eyes lit up as Ethan explained how this real-world example showcased the power of AI. "The same principles can apply to us—whether we're using AI to improve customer experience, optimize our data flow, or manage security risks, the possibilities are endless."

Emily, always eager to contribute, asked, "So what's the first step, Ethan? How do we start integrating AI into our systems?"

Ethan looked around the table, confident in his team's ability to rise to the challenge. "We start by identifying the areas where AI will have the biggest impact. That means looking at what's taking the most time, what's generating the most data, and where we have the most opportunities for growth. We'll start small—pilot a few AI-driven projects, see how they perform, and scale up from there. The goal isn't to overhaul everything overnight. It's to lay a foundation for the future."

He paused for a moment, letting the weight of his words sink in. "AI-driven data analytics isn't just the next step—it's the step that will carry us into the future. It's going to change how we do everything, from customer engagement to internal operations. And if we do this right, we'll not only stay relevant—we'll lead the charge."

As Ethan finished speaking, the team sat in silence, absorbing the magnitude of what he'd just outlined. The future wasn't just coming—it was here. And they were ready to face it, one AI- powered step at a time.

The room was quiet, all eyes on Ethan, as he laid out his vision. It was ambitious, forward- looking, and essential. He knew it wouldn't be easy, but the team was ready. They'd faced challenges before, and they'd overcome them.

"Let's ride this wave together," Ethan finished with a grin, echoing Sarah's words from the night before.

The future was coming fast, but Ethan and his team were ready to meet it head-on.

As the meeting concluded, Ethan leaned back in his chair, a satisfied grin spreading across his face. His team buzzed with energy, animatedly discussing the potential of AI-driven data analytics. "Can you imagine," Jake exclaimed, "a world where we're not just reacting to data but predicting trends before they even happen? It's like having a crystal ball but way cooler and less... mystical!"

"Right?" Emily chimed in. "With AI, we'll finally get to stop playing whack-a-mole with our data issues. Instead, we'll be proactive, like data ninjas ready to strike before problems even arise!"

Ethan chuckled, raising an eyebrow. "Data ninjas, huh? Just remember, with great power comes great responsibility. We don't want to end up like that one superhero movie where the sidekick tries to save the day and just... trips over his own cape."

Mark, always the skeptic, smirked. "I'm just worried we'll end up in a situation where the AI takes over and we're left playing fetch with it, like some overzealous robot dog."

“Hey, at least it would bring us coffee!” Jake shot back. “Imagine a world where the data makes the coffee runs. Now that’s what I call optimizing!”

As laughter filled the room, Ethan couldn’t help but feel a wave of optimism. They were on the brink of something groundbreaking, and with humor to lighten the load, they’d tackle whatever challenges lay ahead.

The future was approaching fast, and Ethan knew they were ready to ride the wave. All they needed was a little laughter and a lot of collaboration. Because in the world of technology, sometimes the best innovation comes from not taking themselves too seriously.

The Journey Ahead

As the dust settled on their final project, Ethan stood at the office window, watching the city lights blink into the night. Each twinkle felt like a beacon of hope, illuminating the path they had travelled.

The skyline, with its towering buildings and shimmering reflections, served as a metaphor for their journey — each light representing a challenge they had faced, a solution they had discovered, and a new opportunity awaiting them. He couldn't help but reflect on how far they had come from those early days when integrating AWS Data Lake and SQL Server felt like scaling a daunting mountain.

Now, with machine learning models predicting customer behaviors and AI-driven analytics guiding their strategic decisions, they had truly come full circle.

The team had grown, not just in technical skill but as individuals. Jake's quirky energy had often lightened the mood during stressful meetings, while Emily's steady hand and methodical approach ensured that no detail was overlooked.

Mark's sharp insights and willingness to challenge the status quo had pushed them to innovate at every turn. Together, they had forged a bond that transcended typical workplace relationships, united by their shared mission to push the boundaries of what was possible in data management.

Ethan understood that technology, for all its complexity and potential, had one constant truth - it was only as powerful as the people who wielded it. He felt immense pride in being surrounded by individuals who embraced change, questioned the norm, and relentlessly sought answers to the question,

"What's next?" This spirit of curiosity and determination had transformed their workplace into a dynamic hub of innovation.

As he closed his laptop for what felt like the thousandth time, he glanced at a post-it on his desk — a small, cheerful reminder from Sarah. The note, written in her distinctive handwriting during one of those late nights, read, "The future isn't something that just happens to you; it's something you build, one decision at a time."

That simple message resonated deeply with him. It encapsulated their journey and the challenges they had tackled together. Every late night spent brainstorming, every coffee- fueled strategy session, every moment of frustration had contributed to this collective achievement.

Ethan smiled as he thought about the journey ahead. The road before them was still lined with challenges — AI ethics, data privacy, and emerging technologies would require them to adapt and evolve. But he felt a renewed sense of excitement about the future. The landscape of data management was constantly shifting, and with it came opportunities to learn, grow, and innovate.

As the city buzzed outside and the quiet of the night settled in, Ethan turned off the light, a sense of exhilaration still humming in his chest. He wondered about the possibilities that awaited them. Each decision they made would shape their future, steering them toward uncharted waters filled with potential.

What's next? - The question lingered in the air, heavy with promise. For the first time in a long time, Ethan didn't worry about the answer. He was ready to embrace it, whatever it may be. The future was bright, and the road ahead, while uncertain, was filled with endless possibilities.

In that moment, he felt a sense of purpose, knowing that whatever challenges lay ahead, they would face them together, fortified by the laughter, camaraderie, and shared dreams that had brought them this far.

The excitement of the unknown was invigorating, and as he stepped away from the window, Ethan knew they were prepared to navigate the waters of the future with confidence, resilience, and a sense of adventure.

Core Concepts In Depth

AWS Data Lake

At the heart of modern data strategy, AWS Data Lake serves as the central hub for managing terabyte-scale data. This technology enables businesses to consolidate vast amounts of structured and unstructured data from various sources, storing it in a central repository. Services like Amazon S3 provide scalable, durable storage, while AWS Glue facilitates data cataloging, making it easier to search and manage metadata.

Tools like Amazon Athena enable users to run real-time analytics and perform queries directly on raw data, without needing to move or transform it first. By leveraging AWS Data Lake, companies can unlock powerful insights through machine learning, AI, and real-time analytics, transforming data into actionable strategies with ease.

AWS Data Lake offers remarkable scalability, making it ideal for organizations handling terabyte-scale or even petabyte-scale data. Its cost-effective pay-as-you-go pricing model helps businesses manage large volumes of data without incurring excessive costs. The flexibility to handle structured, semi-structured, and unstructured data allows companies to manage diverse datasets.

AWS Data Lake's integration with tools like Athena for querying and SageMaker for machine learning enables seamless analytics and AI-driven insights directly on raw data. Additionally, the platform's strong security features, such as encryption, fine-grained access control, and audit logging, ensure that it meets strict compliance and data protection standards.

However, AWS Data Lake is not without its challenges. The initial setup can be complex, especially for teams unfamiliar with AWS's cloud architecture, requiring a significant learning curve. Real-time analytics can face latency issues, particularly when dealing with large datasets distributed across regions.

Furthermore, there is the risk of vendor lock-in, where businesses may become overly reliant on AWS's ecosystem, limiting their ability to shift to other platforms or adopt hybrid solutions.

As data continues to grow at an exponential rate, the future of AWS Data Lake will revolve around even greater scalability, automation, and seamless integration with emerging technologies. With advancements in cloud computing, data lakes will become more self- sufficient, offering real-time auto-scaling and smarter storage management.

Innovations like serverless computing and edge computing will allow businesses to manage and analyze data closer to its source, reducing latency and increasing performance. Additionally, as AI and machine learning evolve, AWS Data Lakes will provide deeper, more sophisticated insights with less human intervention, making data-driven decision-making more automated and predictive.

Looking ahead, as data volumes continue to grow, even AWS's scalable architecture may face challenges in maintaining optimal performance without significantly increasing costs. The demand for real-time analytics and immediate decision-making is also expected to rise, which will push AWS Data Lake to innovate further in reducing data latency and processing times.

SQL Server

While cloud technologies like AWS Data Lake are revolutionizing data storage, SQL Server remains a robust and reliable option for managing relational databases on-premise. SQL Server's ability to handle structured data with complex relationships makes it an indispensable tool for enterprises dealing with transactional systems or highly organized datasets.

When integrated with AWS Data Lake, SQL Server helps organizations manage data across hybrid infrastructures—on-premise and cloud. This combination allows for the efficient processing of large-scale data while maintaining the flexibility to switch between environments based on specific business needs.

Server remains a powerful on-premise solution for managing relational databases. It offers robust transaction processing and data integrity, making it a reliable choice for businesses dealing with highly structured data.

SQL Server's compatibility with AWS Data Lake allows organizations to combine on-premise infrastructure with cloud scalability, giving them the best of both worlds. The SQL querying capabilities are advanced, providing users with the ability to conduct complex operations on their datasets with ease.

One of the major drawbacks of SQL Server is its limited scalability compared to cloud-based solutions. While it excels in structured data management, it is not well-suited for unstructured or semi-structured data.

Managing SQL Server infrastructure requires a dedicated IT team, adding overhead costs for maintenance, updates, and security management. Additionally, as data grows, on-premise servers can become costly to expand and maintain

As hybrid cloud environments gain prominence, SQL Server will continue to evolve by offering deeper integration with cloud platforms like AWS and Azure. The future will likely see SQL Server becoming even more adaptable, allowing seamless transitions between on-premise and cloud environments without performance loss.

With the rise of containerization and microservices architecture, SQL Server could become more modular, enabling organizations to deploy, scale, and manage SQL instances more efficiently across different infrastructures. SQL Server's role in the data ecosystem will remain crucial as relational database management systems adapt to support massive, distributed, and real-time data workloads.

As more organizations move toward cloud-based data strategies, SQL Server's relevance may diminish unless integrated with hybrid or multi-cloud systems. Future challenges will also include managing the increasing complexity of data types and scaling on-premise infrastructure to meet growing demands, all while ensuring cost efficiency.

AI and Machine Learning

In the world of data analytics, AI and machine learning are game-changers. As this book unfolds, AI-driven data analytics becomes a key focus, with Ethan and his team exploring the immense possibilities it opens up. AI algorithms can process terabyte-scale data more efficiently than traditional methods, extracting hidden patterns, automating complex tasks, and making predictive insights possible.

Machine learning models can continuously learn from new data, helping organizations optimize operations, forecast trends, and even automate decision-making processes. Ethan's team frequently discusses how AI can help improve performance, enhance real-time data processing, and reduce manual intervention.

AI and machine learning have the potential to revolutionize data management by offering automation, predictive analytics, and deep insights that were previously unattainable. By analyzing vast datasets in real time, AI-driven solutions can uncover hidden patterns, improve decision-making, and optimize business processes.

The biggest challenge with implementing AI and machine learning is the need for specialized skills and infrastructure. Not all teams have the expertise required to design, train, and deploy AI models effectively. AI-driven solutions can also be resource-intensive, demanding substantial computational power and storage, which increases costs. There is also the risk of bias in machine learning models, which can skew results if not handled properly.

The future of AI and machine learning in data analytics is bright and filled with potential. AI models will continue to get smarter and more self-learning, reducing the need for human intervention in routine data processing tasks.

Autonomous AI systems could handle complex queries, optimize data pipelines in real time, and even offer prescriptive analytics that suggest the best course of action based on predictive insights. Machine learning models will become more democratized, with user- friendly tools enabling non-experts to harness the power of AI for their data needs. AI-driven automation will extend from data analytics to business operations, where AI will optimize processes, reduce costs, and enhance efficiency across entire organizations.

The future of AI in data management will bring more complexity in managing AI systems themselves. Ensuring the transparency and fairness of AI decisions will become a critical issue, especially as regulations around AI ethics and data privacy tighten. As AI adoption grows, balancing innovation with the ethical and legal implications of machine learning will be key challenges for businesses.

Cost Management

Managing the costs of storing and processing data is a critical concern for organizations. Throughout the book, the team delves into strategies for effective cost management. They often compare the traditional on-premise setups, which require significant upfront investment in hardware and maintenance, with AWS's pay-as-you-go model. By using cloud services, businesses can scale up or down based on their needs, eliminating the need for over- provisioning and paying only for what they use.

Through AWS's various pricing tiers and optimization tools, companies can find ways to manage expenses while maintaining high levels of performance and flexibility.

Cost management is a critical advantage of adopting cloud-based solutions like AWS Data Lake. The ability to scale storage and compute power on demand ensures that businesses only pay for what they use, avoiding the high upfront costs associated with traditional infrastructure. In this book, Ethan's team explores ways to optimize costs by using tiered storage options, monitoring usage patterns, and utilizing reserved instances to lower expenses.

Despite these advantages, cloud cost management can become a challenge, particularly as organizations scale. Without proper monitoring and optimization strategies, expenses can spiral out of control due to data ingress and egress fees, underutilized services, or overly complex architectures. Predicting costs can also be difficult, as usage patterns may fluctuate.

The future of cost management in data handling will focus on smarter resource allocation and automated optimization. Tools powered by AI and machine learning will predict resource usage, offering proactive solutions to reduce costs by adjusting storage and compute power dynamically.

Serverless architectures will become increasingly important, allowing businesses to eliminate idle resources and pay only for actual usage. Cost optimization features will be embedded into all aspects of cloud services, from storage to compute to networking, enabling companies to maximize performance while keeping expenses under control. Additionally, advancements in multi-cloud strategies will offer businesses the flexibility to move data and workloads between providers to take advantage of the most cost-effective options.

In the future, as data continues to grow and businesses demand more real-time capabilities, cost management will remain a balancing act. Optimizing performance while controlling costs will require businesses to stay ahead of cloud cost management tools and strategies. Additionally, as multi-cloud and hybrid solutions become more popular, cost management across different platforms will add a new layer of complexity.

Security

In a world where data breaches and cyber threats are constant, security is a top priority. The book explores security challenges associated with moving sensitive data to the cloud, particularly how major financial institutions navigate these risks. AWS offers a robust suite of security features like encryption at rest and in transit, Identity and Access Management (IAM), and multi-factor authentication, ensuring that data remains protected.

Real-world examples highlight how AWS's security services provide the necessary compliance and governance tools to keep data safe, while also being adaptable to the specific requirements of different industries like healthcare, finance, and retail.

In an era of increasing cyber threats, data security is a top priority. AWS

Data Lake offers a comprehensive set of security features, including encryption at rest and in transit, access control policies, and audit logs.

These features help organizations comply with industry regulations and protect their data from unauthorized access. Ethan's team explores real-world security case studies, discussing how large institutions handle cloud security challenges effectively.

As the volume of sensitive data grows and cyber threats become more sophisticated, the future of data security will involve even stronger encryption standards, more granular access controls, and advanced threat detection powered by AI. Zero-trust architectures will become standard, ensuring that no user, system, or device is trusted by default.

However, security in the cloud comes with its own set of challenges. Misconfigurations or weak security protocols can lead to data breaches, which are not only costly but can also damage an organization's reputation. While cloud providers like AWS offer security tools, the responsibility of implementing and managing them correctly falls on the business, requiring specialized knowledge and constant vigilance.

Continuous monitoring and real-time response systems will be powered by machine learning, identifying and neutralizing security risks faster than ever before. Cloud providers like AWS will continue to innovate, offering compliance-as-a-service and automated governance tools that ensure data security without compromising on speed or scalability. Security frameworks will also extend into edge computing environments, providing seamless protection for data processed outside traditional data centers.

The future of data security will be shaped by the increasing sophistication of cyberattacks and the expanding regulatory landscape. Businesses will need to stay proactive, adopting emerging technologies like AI-driven security monitoring and zero-trust architectures to protect against evolving threats. Moreover, with the rise of quantum computing on the horizon, encryption methods used today may become obsolete, requiring businesses to rethink their security strategies.

Mastering The Core Concepts For The Future Of Data

The core concepts explored throughout this book—AWS Data Lake, SQL Server, AI and Machine Learning, Cost Management, and Security — are not just technical tools but pillars of modern data strategy. Together, they form the foundation for handling vast and complex datasets, extracting valuable insights, and ultimately driving business growth in the digital age.

How to Perceive These Concepts

Each of these technologies plays a specific role in an organization's data landscape, and their significance is only growing as data continues to explode in volume and complexity. AWS Data Lake enables businesses to manage terabyte-scale data efficiently, SQL Server provides robust database management for structured data, and AI and machine learning unlock new opportunities for automation and predictive analytics. Cost management ensures that these solutions remain scalable and affordable, while robust security frameworks protect data from the increasing risk of breaches and cyberattacks.

Organizations should perceive these concepts as enablers of innovation. They are not just isolated technologies but interconnected solutions that, when leveraged together, offer transformative potential. Whether you are a data architect, a business leader, or an AI engineer, understanding these tools helps you stay ahead of the curve in a competitive market.

How to Leverage These Concepts

One of the key takeaways from this book is the power of integrating cloud solutions like AWS Data Lake with traditional infrastructure such as SQL Server. Organizations can harness the strengths of both on-premise and cloud environments to create hybrid data systems that offer flexibility, scalability, and cost savings.

AI and machine learning are no longer buzzwords; they are practical tools that provide actionable insights and drive automation. Organizations should invest in AI technologies to optimize processes, reduce human error, and uncover patterns in data that can improve decision-making and performance.

Cost management is crucial for sustainable growth. By leveraging tools like AWS Cost Explorer, businesses can track and optimize cloud expenditures, ensuring that they are not overpaying for resources or services they don't need. Understanding pricing models, using reserved instances, and monitoring usage patterns are essential for keeping costs in check.

Security should be woven into the fabric of any data strategy. Implement multi-layered security protocols, ensure proper encryption, and establish strong access controls to protect sensitive data. A lapse in security can not only harm the business but also its customers and stakeholders.

What Not to Do: Avoiding Pitfalls that Could Harm Humans

While AI and machine learning can streamline processes and reduce manual effort, over- reliance on automation without proper human oversight can lead to unintended consequences. Algorithms are only as good as the data they are trained on, and biased data can result in unfair outcomes, especially in critical areas like healthcare, finance, and employment. Always ensure ethical considerations are factored into AI development.

With the increasing volume of sensitive data being processed, overlooking data security could lead to devastating breaches. Businesses must not assume that cloud providers alone are responsible for security. Shared responsibility models mean that organizations need to actively manage their own data governance and compliance.

It's easy to get caught up in the excitement of new technologies, but businesses should be cautious about adopting tools without a clear strategy. Implementing AI or machine learning without understanding how they align with business objectives can waste resources and potentially lead to decisions based on incomplete or inaccurate data.

While cost management is important, cutting costs in areas like security or infrastructure can lead to larger problems down the line. Balancing cost savings with performance and security ensures that the organization remains resilient and adaptable.

Final Thoughts

The future of data management is bright but comes with its own set of challenges. By embracing the core concepts discussed in this book, organizations can position themselves for long-term success. However, leveraging these technologies responsibly is key to ensuring that data-driven strategies benefit both businesses and society at large. Ethical considerations, security protocols, and a focus on continuous learning will allow companies to unlock the full potential of these transformative technologies without harming the people they serve.

Thank You To The Business Fame

I would like to extend my heartfelt gratitude to The Business Fame for their support and commitment to fostering entrepreneurship. It is often the small beginnings that lead to significant outcomes—outcomes that are worth the risks we take. Throughout our journey in the entrepreneurial landscape, we have worked tirelessly toward a shared goal: to showcase, cater to, and deliver valuable industry insights to businesses of all sizes.

The Business Fame (TBF) stands as a beacon for entrepreneurs and ventures at every stage, helping them gain visibility and connect with potential clients, industry leaders, and like- minded individuals. As a Business-to-Business (B2B) magazine, TBF serves as an invaluable platform for sharing knowledge, insights, and analyses that drive business outreach and technological advancement.

In this data-driven era, TBF provides a treasure trove of information, meticulously sourced and verified to ensure the highest quality. By offering precise insights into industry-specific trends and news, TBF has created a space where businesses can not only advertise their products and services but also enhance their brand presence and awareness.

The diverse audience that TBF attracts from experts and industry leaders to everyday individuals and potential clients — benefits immensely from the magazine's thorough coverage of market trends, industry knowledge, and future predictions. This platform equips businesses with the information necessary to strategize growth effectively.

Thank you, The Business Fame, for being an essential partner in this journey and for your dedication to empowering entrepreneurs. Together, we will continue to illuminate the path to success for many in the business community.

Acknowledgement To Scriberlee

I extend my heartfelt gratitude to Scriberlee, a remarkable branding firm with a dual presence in Singapore and India. Your commitment to brand building, content writing, and training has been instrumental in my journey. Featured in Forbes India for your dedication to quality content, Scriberlee is not just a service provider; you are a partner in transformation.

Your team's innovative approach has helped brands, coaches, mentors, and trainers stand out in a competitive market. You challenge the status quo, proving that great branding doesn't conform to norms but instead breaks barriers and creates impact. With a focus on creating that "wow effect," you have elevated my brand's energy through thorough brand research, identity development, captivating content writing, and stunning graphic and web design.

I deeply appreciate the attention to detail you bring, considering every angle, even those I may have overlooked. Your philosophy of maintaining ideas that are always "on the boil," much like your excellent coffee, reflects your vibrant and dynamic spirit. The regular, constructive feedback you provide keeps me aligned with my goals while pushing the boundaries of what's possible.

Thank you for assisting me in understanding who I am and helping me become who I aspire to be. Whether over a drink, a phone conversation, or a workshop, your support has been invaluable, and I look forward to our continued journey together.

Thank You Note To Readers

Dear Readers,

Thank you for taking the time to embark on this journey with me through the intricate world of data and technology. Your commitment to understanding these concepts is not just commendable but essential in today's fast-paced, data-driven landscape.

I hope that the insights and knowledge shared in this book have sparked your curiosity and inspired you to explore the transformative power of data in your personal and professional lives. Your willingness to learn and adapt is what will drive innovation and shape the future.

As you move forward, I encourage you to apply what you've learned, question the status quo, and continue to seek out new opportunities for growth and understanding.

Thank you once again for being a part of this adventure. Your engagement and interest mean the world to me!

With gratitude,
Vijay Panwar

www.ingramcontent.com/pod-product-compliance
Ingram Content Group UK Ltd.
Pitfield, Milton Keynes, MK11 3LW, UK
UKHW062312290726
14090UKWH00018B/1018

9 798895 884126